תורה אור
ויושט המלר לאסתר

JOURNEY
OF THE SOUL

תורה אור
ויושט המלך לאסתר

JOURNEY
OF THE SOUL

a chasidic discourse by
Rabbi Schneur Zalman of Liadi
זצוקללה״ה נבג״מ זי״ע
The Alter Rebbe

•

translation and commentary
by
Rabbi Ari Sollish

KEHOT PUBLICATION SOCIETY
770 Eastern Parkway / Brooklyn, New York 11213

JOURNEY
OF THE SOUL

Published and Copyrighted © 2003
Second Printing 2004
by
KEHOT PUBLICATION SOCIETY
770 Eastern Parkway / Brooklyn, New York 11213
(718) 774-4000 / Fax (718) 774-2718

Orders:
291 Kingston Avenue / Brooklyn, New York 11213
(718) 778-0226 / Fax (718) 778-4148
www.kehotonline.com

ISBN 0-8266-0465-X

Manufactured in the United States of America

CONTENTS

SPONSORED BY
A GENEROUS GRANT FROM THE

GANSBOURG

GNIWISCH

KRASNANSKY

FAMILIES

PREFACE

We are proud to present *Journey of the Soul*, the first discourse of Rabbi Schneur Zalman of Liadi to be published in the acclaimed Chasidic Heritage Series. The discourse, which opens with the words *Vayoshet Hamelech L'Esther*, was originally printed in Hebrew in Rabbi Schneur Zalman's anthology of discourses, *Torah Or*. It appears here in English for the very first time.

The discourses in *Torah Or* are well known for their unique ability to probe into the heart and psyche of man, and from there to provide direction to one's divine service. As the *Tzemach Tzedek*, grandson of Rabbi Schneur Zalman, writes: "In [these discourses], those who seek G-d and the Torah of Truth will find rest for their souls."[1] The present offering, *Journey of the Soul*, is no exception. It outlines the struggle of the G-dly soul against the materialistic elements of man, and illuminates the most assured path one can take toward spiritual fulfillment.

Journey of the Soul is also a Purim discourse. It is set against the backdrop of Queen Esther's petition to King Ahasuerus to save her people from Haman's evil plot, which, as Rabbi Schneur Zalman explains, alludes to the soul's petition to draw near to G-d, away from the evil influences that threaten its wholesomeness.

Rabbi Ari Sollish translated the discourse and added extensive annotation and commentary to clarify the obscure concepts referred to in the text. The Hebrew text has been retypeset with Hebrew vowel marks and broken into chapters to further enhance this volume's usability. A brief biography of the

---

1. This is an excerpt from a letter dated 3 *Shevat* 5597 (1837). The letter is printed in *Igrot Kodesh* of the *Tzemach Tzedek*, pp. 334-5, as well as in the introduction to (the first edition of) *Derech Mitzvotecha*.

author's life and his published works have been added as an appendix.

Special thanks are due to *Heichal Menachem,* whose publication of this discourse in the *Chasidut Mevueret* series aided in its translation and annotation. Thanks are also due to Rabbis Yosef B. Friedman, Avraham D. Vaisfiche and Dovid Olidort for their editorial assistance.

Kehot Publication Society

14 Adar I, 5763

RABBI SCHNEUR ZALMAN OF LIADI
זצוקללה"ה נבג"מ זי"ע
5505–5573 (1745–1812)

Facsimile of handwritten manuscript by Rabbi Schneur Zalman

INTRODUCTION
AND
SUMMARY

INTRODUCTION AND SUMMARY

Rabbi Menachem Mendel of Lubavitch, the *Tzemach Tzedek*, writes: The love expressed in "Besides You I wish for nothing,"[1] means that one should desire nothing other than G-d, not even "Heaven" or "earth," i.e., Higher *Gan Eden* or Lower *Gan Eden*, for these were created with a mere *yud*...[2] The love is to be directed to Him alone, to His very Being and Essence. This was actually heard from my master and teacher, Rabbi Schneur Zalman, when he was in a state of *d'veikut* [spiritual ecstacy] and would exclaim:

I want nothing at all! I don't want Your *Gan Eden*, I don't want Your *Olam Haba*... I want nothing but You alone! —*Hayom Yom, 18th of Kislev*

The *Tzemach Tzedek* employs the phrase "*was* heard" to indicate that this was not an isolated statement. Rabbi Schneur Zalman, in fact, would say this quite often...
—*Kuntres Purim Katan 5752*

A RENOWNED EXPERT IN THE MYSTICAL, KABBALISTIC DIMENSIONS of the Torah, as well as its "revealed" aspects, Rabbi Schneur Zalman of Liadi[3] well understood and appreciated the various metaphysical realms that exist beyond our world. There are the "worlds" of *Atzilut, Beriah* and *Yetzirah*, the angelic "chambers," the infinite levels of Paradise (*Gan Eden*). Yet, to meditate upon these sublime levels

---

1. Psalms 73:25.

2. The Divine Essence-name, *Havaya* (the Tetragrammaton), is the source of all creation. *Olam Haba*, spiritual Hereafter, including *Gan Eden*, was created from the first (and smallest) letter—*yud*—of the Name.

3. Known as the Rav (Rabbi), and amongst Chasidim as the Alter Rebbe (Elder Rabbi); 1745-1812. Founder and leader of Chabad-Chasidism; author of *Likkutei Amarim (Tanya)*, an authoritative revision of *Shulchan Aruch, Torah Or, Likkutei Torah*, etc. (A detailed biography is currently available, published by Kehot, 2001.)

and thereby "experience" spiritual awareness did not satisfy Rabbi Schneur Zalman. For to perceive these supernal sights is to merely catch a glimpse of spirituality; Rabbi Schneur Zalman wanted nothing but G-d Himself.[4]

It is not surprising, then, that much of his philosophy and meditation reflects this sentiment. Indeed, in many of his teachings, Rabbi Schneur Zalman explains that although the search for spirituality is a worthy endeavor, ultimately, G-d must be the focus of our efforts.[5] The *maamar* presented here, entitled *Journey of the Soul*, is one such example where this idea is developed.

HISTORICAL BACKGROUND

The discourse, which opens with the verse "*Vayoshet Hamelech L'Esther*" from *Megillat Esther* (the Book of Esther), was delivered by Rabbi Schneur Zalman on Purim, 5560 (1800), in the city of Liozna, and was transcribed shortly thereafter by his brother, Rabbi Yehuda Leib. In 5597 (1837), the *Tzemach Tzedek* published this *maamar*, together with hundreds of other discourses of Rabbi Schneur Zalman, under the title "*Torah Or.*"[6]

To better understand the backdrop of this discourse, it is necessary to examine the historical context in which it was said—a time that was quite momentous for Rabbi Schneur Zalman.

Nearly a year and a half before, on the day after Sukkot 5559 (1798), Rabbi Schneur Zalman was arrested and taken to Petersburg, where he was imprisoned in the Peter–Paul fortress under charges of high treason. Fifty-three days later, on the 19th of Kislev, after undergoing fierce examination, Rabbi Schneur Zalman was found to be innocent of all charges and was released. From that point on, his activities as leader of the relatively new Chabad move-

---

4. However brilliant and resplendent, the spiritual realms are but reflections of G-dly light—"palatial chambers" demonstrating the King's grandeur. Though visitors to these chambers are impressed with glimpses of His majesty and awesomeness, it is obviously not the same as being with the King Himself. One whose focus is on the King will surely disregard these chambers, finding them to be somewhat of a distraction—despite their grandness.

5. This idea has since become a central theme in Chabad-Chasidut philosophy, echoed throughout the discourses of Rabbi Schneur Zalman's successors.

6. P. 93d ff.

ment gained new vigor, and there was a marked change in the Chasidut that he said. While the *maamarim* of the past were relatively brief, with relatively few explanations of difficult concepts, the post-Petersburg discourses were much longer, with many more explanations.[7]

Thus began a new era in the dissemination of Chasidic teachings—a climate in which the present discourse was taught.

GENERAL OUTLINE

Like many festival discourses, *Journey of the Soul* contains two elements: it is of a holiday theme, with the purpose of exploring the deeper dimension of Purim, yet it also contains profound lessons and insights that are of timeless benefit for our spiritual service.

Before explaining the spiritual significance of Purim, the discourse examines a broader topic—the perilous trek of the soul in its quest for G-d and spirituality: from its initial entrapment within the physical, narcissistic body and the daily grind of material life, to its bitter struggle with and ultimate conquest of these negative elements, and finally, to its uniting completely with G-d. The discourse does this by describing at length the spiritual condition of the Jewish people in three distinct periods: Exile, Shabbat and Festivals, and the Messianic Era.

Exile, or *galut*, in which we currently find ourselves, is marked by a concealment of G-dliness. It is a time when G-d's "face" is hidden from creation, when we cannot perceive the divine force that guides our lives and perpetually animates all of existence. A time, it seems, when we are without spiritual direction, and instead, are merely being swept away by societal currents.

But amidst the darkness of exile a window opens for us, a window that looks out upon the brilliant radiance of divinity and allows the warm rays of spirituality to shine in our hearts. This "window" is the Shabbat and festivals, when G-d breaks out of hiding and manifests His radiance upon us, lifting us out of the doldrums of our

---

7. Although Rabbi Schneur Zalman's release from imprisonment in 1798 initiated a new phase in the dissemination of Chasidut, the most marked change occurred after he returned from his second arrest in 1801 and settled in Liadi. See *Torat Shalom*, p. 26 ff.; *Kuntres Limud Hachasidut*, p. 9.

daily, material battles, injecting us with new vigor and excitement in our divine service, granting us spiritual "vision."

Yet, the *maamar* says, there will come a time when the glow of the Shabbat and festivals will seem so faint, so dim. For when Moshiach comes, *G-d's Essence*—not just His radiance—will be revealed throughout creation, for "all flesh" to see. This will be the ultimate time, the culmination of all of our toil during exile, the universal fulfillment of what Rabbi Schneur Zalman so often wished for: G-d Himself will finally be manifest.

This describes the interplay of G-d and creation on a macrocosmic level. The same three stages also exist on a microcosmic plane, in the personal, spiritual journey of a soul in exile.

Initially, one's soul may be lost within the tumultuousness of physical life, trapped as it were amidst the daily struggle to survive in a wholly materialistic environment, finding no voice with which to express its spiritual longings. Thus, it is in a personal "exile."

There are times, however, when the soul breaks free of its earthly tether and begins to express its intrinsic love and yearning toward G-d. This can be done in two distinct manners. One is through meditating upon the greatness of G-d as He creates and sustains the world, which in turn rouses the soul with a burning love and desire for G-dliness, to experience divine radiance. The other is accomplished through meditating upon the Essence of G-d, as He is completely beyond creation. This inflames the soul with a passion and longing not for G-dliness, but for G-d Himself—"I want nothing but You alone."

All of this is presented by Rabbi Schneur Zalman in the context of Purim, in the course of explaining various verses and themes of the *Megillah*, ultimately demonstrating how in a deeper sense the holiday of Purim embodies the Messianic ideal—when the soul is bound completely with G-d, and He is fully manifest.

DUELING SCEPTERS

The discourse begins by noting some textual differences between two similar episodes recounted in the *Megillah*. Twice, the scripture tells us that King Ahasuerus extended his gold scepter to Queen Esther. The first reference is found in the fifth chapter, where following Esther's learning of Haman's plot to destroy the Jewish people, G-d forbid, she decides to venture to the palace uninvited and see the king. At that point we are told: "When the king saw Queen Esther standing in the courtyard, she found favor in his eyes. The king extended to Esther the golden scepter that was in his hand, and Esther approached and touched the tip of the scepter."[8]

The second reference comes in Chapter Eight, after Haman's plot is exposed by Esther and he is executed. There, the text reads: "Esther again spoke before the king and fell before his feet, and she cried and begged him to nullify the evil decree of Haman the Agagite and his plot that he had plotted against the Jews. The king extended the golden scepter to Esther, and Esther rose and stood before the king."[9]

The *maamar* thus notes that in the first source, the verse emphasizes the fact that the gold scepter was in the king's hand, and that Esther only touched the tip of the scepter—two points that are omitted in the second reference.

Furthermore, the relevance of this story to our present-day spiritual service is questioned.

From that point on, the *maamar* strips the story of Esther from its basic, literal reading, and proceeds to develop and expound the more sublime messages contained in the *Megillah*.

SUBTLE SYMBOLISM

Esther is a symbol of the G-dly concealment during *galut*. This is true both on a global scale and on a personal level: divinity is not blatantly manifest in creation, nor do our souls find a consistent outlet for their spiritual longings. This is in stark contrast with the Messianic Era, when G-dliness will be revealed and will shine throughout existence.

But, there are times even during our current exile when we are given a taste of spirituality and the Time to Come. On the Shabbat and festivals, G-d "lifts the veil," so to speak, and allows His radiance to shine upon creation, lifting us up from the grips of materiality and infusing our divine service with added love and enthusiasm.

---

8. Esther 5:2.   9. Ibid. 8:3-4.

RISING SMOKE

This "elevation process" is intimated in the following verse from King Solomon's Song of Songs[10]: "Who is this rising from the wilderness, like columns of smoke, perfumed with myrrh and frankincense, with every powder of the merchant?"

Initially, our souls are found in the barren "wilderness" of physicality, a place devoid of any overt trace of G-dliness. On the Shabbat and festivals, however, G-dliness is manifest in creation, enabling us to "ascend" from this "wilderness." When the soul is activated during these special times, it is able to overwhelm and "burn" (destroy) the negative elements that it was previously involved with, irrespective of how blatant or subtle those elements may be. This "burning" procedure produces "spiritual smoke," just as fire's consumption of an element opposite itself—moisture—produces physical smoke.

G-D VS. G-DLINESS

Yet, the discourse says, regardless of the degree to which the soul is inspired on the Shabbat and festivals to love G-d, and irrespective of how high the soul climbs in its spiritual journey, it still pales in comparison with the awesome, cataclysmic shift that will occur in the Messianic Era. For then, not only will G-dliness be manifest in creation, but G-d Himself will be revealed for "all flesh to see."

What is the difference between "G-dliness" and "G-d Himself"?

"G-dliness" refers to spiritual "light," various effusions of divinity that are essential in the process of perpetually creating and sustaining all of existence. Thus, though representing extremely sublime levels, they are by their very definition not G-d, but rather tools through which our reality came into being.

G-d, on the other hand, is completely beyond creation. Furthermore, He is beyond any "labels" or descriptions—even the label "beyond creation"—for one can only describe that which is in the realm of comprehension. G-d, Who created that realm, is certainly not "contained in" or "limited to" such a realm.

And when Moshiach comes, G-d Himself—the very G-d that is completely removed from creation—will be manifest in this world.

---

10. 3:6.

MESSIANIC MOMENT

How will this be possible?

In the past, divinity has been able to be revealed when the negative, impure elements have been subdued. Never, though, have these elements themselves been totally transformed to goodness. In the times of Moshiach, "the darkness itself will turn to light"—thus G-d will be able to be manifest in creation.

In this vein, we can understand the difference between the "tip" of the scepter and the "entire" scepter. The "tip" refers to the divine emanations that relate to creation, and that can be experienced periodically in our current condition. The "entire" scepter relates to G-d Himself, Who will be manifest in the Messianic Age.

PURIM TRANSFORMATION

The *maamar* thus explains why amongst all of the festivals, only Purim will not be abolished when Moshiach comes.[11] The divine light that shines during the festivals is but a faint glow compared to the great manifestation of G-d of the Messianic Era, and will be utterly suffused in its great splendor. Purim, however, is of similar quality to that awesome time, for it too is marked by "the transformation of darkness to light," represented by the complete change of King Ahasuerus' heart.

HALACHAH AND HUMILITY

The same is true with *halachah* (Jewish law). *Halachah* is the will and wisdom of G-d, garbed in mundane, physical matters. When one deciphers *halachah*, one is essentially taking a scenario that appears to have no spiritual connection and transforming it into a vehicle to express the divine will and wisdom—another example of "transforming darkness to light." Thus, the Talmud states: "Jewish law will never be abolished in the Time to Come."[12]

Why, then, do we not see G-d every time we occupy ourselves with the study of *halachah*?

It is our sins and arrogance that create a "wall" and barrier that prevents us from perceiving the power of our Torah-study. When we tear down these walls, breaking the haughty spirit of our heart and truly developing a feeling of humility, we may then experience G-d.

---

11. *Midrash Mishlei* 9:2.   12. Jerusalem Talmud, *Megillah* 1:5.

ESTHER'S STAND

The discourse concludes by explaining the difference between Esther's two appearances before the king in the above light. Initially, Esther stood in the king's courtyard, yearning to see the king, symbolizing the soul's primitive spiritual approach, when it is still connected with negativity. Then, the soul may touch just the "tip" of the scepter, receiving the divine inspiration that is granted on the Shabbat and festivals. Eventually, however, Esther came to the king's actual residence. There, she "wept and implored him to avert the evil [intention] of Haman"—representing the cry of the soul to rid itself of the arrogance that impedes G-dly revelation. When it has accomplished that—transforming the "darkness" of ego into the "light" of spiritual sensitivity—then, "Esther arose and stood before the king"; the soul may truly receive its one wish: "I want nothing but you alone!"

*   *   *

The same year that this *maamar* was said, Rabbi Schneur Zalman said another discourse entitled "*Kol Hamo'adim B'telim*," which explains many of the concepts presented here in greater depth, but in a more esoteric, Kabbalistic style.[13]

In 5586 or 5587 (1826 or 1827) Rabbi DovBer,[14] Rabbi Schneur Zalman's son, taught the *maamar* "*Vayoshet Hamelech L'Esther*,"[15] adding some new concepts and in general giving very extensive explanations, as was his style.[16] In fact, much of the explanatory footnotes and commentary found in the present rendition of the *maamar* are based on Rabbi DovBer's discourse.

In *Or HaTorah* by the *Tzemach Tzedek*,[17] the discourse is

---

13. Printed in *Maamarei Admur Hazaken Al Hatorah v'Hamo'adim*, vol. II, p. 394 ff.

14. Known amongst Chasidim, from the times of the *Tzemach Tzedek* on, as the *Mitteler Rebbe* (the "Middle Rebbe"); 1773-1827. Second leader of the Chabad dynasty.

15. *Maamarei   Admur   Ha'emtza'ee,*

Nevi'im u'Ketuvim, p. 378 ff.

16. Rabbi DovBer's discourses were considerably lengthier than those of his father, and generally contained greater "breadth" of thought.

17. Rabbi Menachem Mendel of Lubavitch (1789-1866), third leader of Chabad. Son-in-law of Rabbi DovBer and grandson of Rabbi Schneur Zalman.

printed with parenthetical glosses interspersed throughout the text, and is followed by several additional pages of commentary, explaining various concepts found in the *maamar* in mystical terms.[18]

And in *Pelach Harimon*, by the great Kabbalist and Chasid Rabbi Hillel of Paritch,[19] there appears a discourse of the same title, heard from the *Tzemach Tzedek* in 5616 (1856), that bears close resemblance to Rabbi Schneur Zalman's discourse and contains additional commentary and explanation from Rabbi Hillel.[20]

Obviously, poring through these sources would prove to be the most assured path to full comprehension of the discourse. Since, however, this is quite a daunting task, we have looked through the many references and have selected those explanations and commentary that we believe will enhance the reader's comprehension of the concepts found in the *maamar*, and have presented them here in the commentary and footnotes. This is in addition to the extensive commentary and explanation of basic (and not so basic) Chasidic and Kabbalistic concepts, culled from the vast wealth of Chasidic teaching of the past two and a half centuries—a feature that has become the hallmark of the Chasidic Heritage Series. We trust that the reader will find the current presentation to be a worthy addition to this fine series, and yet another step forward in the dissemination of Chasidut.

NOTE ON THE HEBREW TEXT: In vowelizing the Hebrew words in this edition we have followed the grammatical rules of the Holy Tongue, which occasionally differ from the traditional or colloquial pronunciation.

---

18. *Or HaTorah, Megillat Esther*, p. 111 ff.

19. 1795-1864. One of the great Chasidim (followers) of the *Mitteler Rebbe* and *Tzemach Tzedek*, and exponent of their discourses.

20. *Pelach Harimon, Shemot*, p. 386 ff.

TRANSLATION
AND
COMMENTARY

"The king extended the golden scepter to Esther, and Esther rose
and stood before the king..."[1]

We find a few discrepancies between our verse and a similar one
in a previous chapter. Earlier in the *Megillah*, it says that "the king
extended [to Esther] the golden scepter *that was in his hand*."[2] Here,
however, this point is omitted. Also, before it is written that Esther
"touched the *tip* of the scepter,"[3] whereas from our verse it would
seem that he gave her the *entire* scepter.[4]

Furthermore, what is the timeless message contained in this
story?[5]

2.

MYSTICAL ESTHER—CONCEALMENT

[To understand all of this, we must first explain the mystical meaning of the word Esther:]

During *galut* (exile), the Jewish people are called "Esther,"[6] in
the sense of concealment [of G-dliness], as we find in the verse,
"And I will utterly hide ("*haster astir*") My face on that day."[7]

The "face" of G-d—referring to the divine presence, as it says,

---

1. Esther 8:4.

2. Ibid. 5:2.

3. Ibid.

4. Simply, this discrepancy could be resolved by noting the distinction between
the two circumstances. The first time Esther approached Kind Ahasuerus, she did
so without prior notification. She was
therefore standing in the "courtyard of
the king" for fear of her life. Thus, it
was sufficient for the king to extend the
scepter in a manner that would merely
allow her to touch its tip. The second

time Esther went before the king, as per
his invitation, she "fell at his feet and
wept." It was only the proper courtesy,
then, for the king to help her stand by
giving her the entire scepter. (*Maamarei
Admur Ha'emtza'ee, Nevi'im-Ketuvim*, p.
378.)

5. "Torah is eternal" (*Tanya*, beg. Chapter 17; *Kuntres Acharon* 160a). Mai-
monides writes in his Thirteen Principles
of Faith, "This Torah will not be ex-
changed nor will there be another Torah
[given] from the Creator..." Chasidut explains that this refers to every aspect of
Torah: every *mitzvah*, every story and in-

וַיּוֹשֶׁט הַמֶּלֶךְ לְאֶסְתֵּר אֵת שַׁרְבִיט הַזָּהָב וַתָּקָם אֶסְתֵּר
וַתַּעֲמוֹד לִפְנֵי הַמֶּלֶךְ וגו'.

לְהָבִין עִנְיַן הַשִּׁינוּיִים שֶׁבֵּין פָּרָשָׁה זוֹ לַפָּרָשָׁה
שֶׁלְּמַעְלָה דְּשָׁם נֶאֱמַר וַיּוֹשֶׁט הַמֶּלֶךְ אֶת שַׁרְבִיט הַזָּהָב
אֲשֶׁר בְּיָדוֹ. וְגַם שָׁם נֶאֱמַר וַתִּגַּע בְּרֹאשׁ הַשַּׁרְבִיט. וְכָאן
מַשְׁמָע שֶׁנָּתַן לָהּ כָּל הַשַּׁרְבִיט.

וְגַם לְהָבִין עִנְיָן זֶה בְּכָל זְמַן מַהוּ.

ב.

הִנֵּה כְּנֶסֶת יִשְׂרָאֵל נִקְרֵאת בְּשֵׁם אֶסְתֵּר עַל שֵׁם וְאָנֹכִי
הַסְתֵּר אַסְתִּיר פָּנַי בַּיּוֹם הַהוּא.

כִּי פְּנֵי ה' שֶׁהוּא גִּילּוּי שְׁכִינָתוֹ כְּמוֹ שֶׁכָּתוּב יָאֵר ה'

---

deed, every detail of Torah, has its parallel in the divine service of every single
Jew, living in any time and in any place.
Thus, the story of Purim, including the
details concerning Esther and the scepter,
must contain a lesson for us all.

6. See *Shemot Rabbah* 30:4.

7. Deuteronomy 31:18.
ESTHER—SPIRITUAL CONCEALMENT:
Chullin 139b states: "From where in the
Torah is [the story of] Esther derived
(that G-d's face will be concealed at that
time and many terrible tragedies will be-
fall Israel—Rashi)? From the verse, 'And I

will surely have concealed ('*haster astir*')
my face on that day.'"

The word "Esther" is etymologically
connected with the word *haster*, concealment. The Talmud therefore "derives" the
pre-miracle portion of the story of Esther
(the decree, the hardships) from the verse
that depicts G-dly concealment. The *maamar* takes this concept a step further, explaining that this verse describes not only
the physical condition of Israel in Esther's
time, but also the spiritual condition of Israel throughout the *entire* exile, for during
exile we are unable to perceive G-dliness,
due to its obfuscation.

"may G-d shine His countenance ("face") upon you"[8]—is now, during exile, hidden, as is intimated in the words *ba'yom ha'hu* ("on that day"). (*Yom ha'hu* ("that day") connotes divine radiance (*yom*) that is not present and manifest, while *yom ha'zeh* ("this day") [connotes divine radiance that is manifest].)[9]

More specifically, this concealment exists within the soul of every single Jew.[10]

When the "spark of G-dliness" that is the soul is buried and garbed in [coarse,] physical thought, speech and action, the divine radiance cannot reside and be manifest within one's being.[11] Consequently, one will not be filled with the burning desire to cleave to G-d with an open heart, lacking the kind of love that has a firm grasp and fix on one's mind and heart. One's love toward G-d will instead be "encompassing from above (*makif*)" [signifying a type of love that exists solely on a subconscious level].[12] This [subliminal]

---

8. Numbers 6:22.

FACE OF G-D: Scripture often uses anthropomorphic terminology when discussing G-d. The reason for this is simple: As created, finite beings, our perception is limited in scope; we can only relate to things that exist in our environment and that we have experienced. Thus, to understand—and certainly to explain—sublime, esoteric, G-dly ideas, scripture reverts to terminology that we are most comfortable with, and assigns "physical" attributes to wholly spiritual concepts. (See *Chovot Halevavot, Shaar Hayichud* ch. 10; *Rambam, Hilchot Yesodei Hatorah* 1:7-12, and *Moreh Nevuchim* 1:26, 33, 35 ff. and 46.)

For example, when scripture speaks of the "arm of G-d," it refers not to a literal arm, G-d forbid (for G-d is not confined to the human form), but rather to G-d's might. The parallel is obvious: Just as the human arm yields man's greatest strength, similarly G-d's "arm" represents His might and power.

The same is true regarding the phrase

quoted by our *maamar*, the "face of G-d." Man's face is virtually a window into his soul—it is the mind and heart's tool of expression and communication. Confusion, enlightenment, pain, ecstasy—indeed, virtually all of man's myriad of deep, inner feelings—are projected and expressed on his face.

So in describing such spiritual concepts as revelation and expression, the best anthropomorphic example is that of the face, the one part of man that visibly demonstrates and reveals to others what is being felt within. Thus, the verses that refer to the "face of G-d" are in reality discussing the act in which G-d is revealing and expressing Himself to creation. (Cf. *Moreh Nevuchim* 1:37.)

[There are other instances where the term "face of G-d" is used to denote divine revelation. One such example: On the verse (Deuteronomy 16:16, "Three times a year all your males should appear before G-d (*p'nei Hashem*)," our sages comment (*Chagigah* 4b): "Just as one came to be seen [by G-d], so too one

פָּנָיו אֵלֶיךָ הוּא עַכְשָׁיו בִּזְמַן הַגָּלוּת מְסוּתֶרֶת בִּבְחִינַת
בַּיּוֹם הַהוּא (כִּי יוֹם הַהוּא מוֹרֶה עַל יוֹם שֶׁאֵינוֹ נִרְאֶה
וְנִגְלָה מַה שֶׁאֵין כֵּן יוֹם הַזֶּה).

וְדֶרֶךְ פְּרָט בְּכָל נֶפֶשׁ מִיִשְׂרָאֵל

הִנֵּה כַּאֲשֶׁר בְּחִינַת נִצּוֹץ נַפְשׁוֹ הָאֱלֹהִית הוּא מְכוּסֶּה
וּמְלוּבָּשׁ בִּלְבוּשֵׁי מַחֲשָׁבָה דִּבּוּר מַעֲשֶׂה הַגַּשְׁמִיִּים וְאֵין
אוֹר ה' שׁוֹרֶה וּמִתְגַּלֶּה בּוֹ לִהְיוֹת נִתְפָּס וְנִקְבָּע
בְּמוֹחוֹ וְלִבּוֹ הָאַהֲבָה לַה' לְדָבְקָה בּוֹ בְּהִתְגַּלּוּת הַלֵּב כִּי
אִם בְּחִינַת מַקִּיף עָלָיו מִלְמַעְלָה נִקְרָא בְּחִינַת אַהֲבָה זוֹ

---

came to see [the 'face of G-d,' G-dly manifestation]." Hence, the Sages interpret *p'nei Hashem* (the "face of G-d") as divine revelation. (*Maamarei Admur Ha'emtza'ee*, ibid, p. 379.)]

For a more elaborate discussion of this topic, see Schochet, *Mystical Concepts in Chassidism*, ch. 1 (*Anthropomorphism and Metaphors*).

9. ZEH AND HU: *Zeh* ("this") is the pronoun used when the subject of reference is present or near in place, time or thought. *Hu* ("that") is used when the subject is farther away or less immediately under observation. Thus, the spiritual implication of the phrase *yom ha'zeh* is that the divine radiance (*yom*, "day") is "immediate" and manifest, while *yom ha'hu* implies that this radiance is "distant" and hidden.

10. Once the *maamar* has explained how in a general sense, G-dliness is not manifest during the exile, it then proceeds to explain how this concealment exists on a

personal level, within each and every one of us.

11. For, as stated in *Chovot Halevavot* (introduction to *Shaar Ahavat Hashem*), "It is impossible for 'love of the Creator' and 'love of the world' to co-exist in the same heart."

See also *Tanya*, Chapter 10: "According to the measure of love one has for G-d, so is the measure of hatred one has for those elements that oppose G-dliness ... One who does not absolutely despise [carnal pleasures] must still have a trace of love and pleasure for them."

12. MAKIF: Lit., "encompassing." Though Chasidut uses the term "*makif*" (encompassing) to describe this love, it is not to be understood in a physical, spatial sense—that somehow this love of G-d *surrounds* the person. Rather it is used figuratively, to indicate an element existent in man yet not consciously sensed or perceived. See below, footnotes 14 and 15.

kind of love is called "Esther," or hidden (*ahavah mesuteret*), similar to the concealment expressed in the phrase "*ba'yom ha'hu.*"[13]

[In Kabbalah,] this "hidden love" of G-d is called *nekuda be'heichala,* "a point within an expanse,"[14] for hidden deep within the heart of every Jewish soul—without exception—is love for G-d.[15] The extent one *reveals* this quintessential love, however, is dependant on the individual.[16]

THE MESSIANIC REVOLUTION

[All of this describes the state of affairs during exile.] In the days of Moshiach, however, man will become more refined,[17] and consequently, "The glory of the L-rd shall be revealed, and together all flesh will see [that the mouth of the L-rd has spoken]."[18] "And it will be said on that day: Behold, this is our G-d in whom we put our hope [that He will deliver us].'"[19]

In that time, there will be such a revelation of divine radiance that it will even have a firm grasp and fix on the mortal mind and intellect, "and all flesh will see" this with physical, tangible vision. Then, "our G-d" will be to us as *zeh*, revealed and manifest, for *zeh*

---

13. AHAVAH MESUTERET: Lit., "hidden love." Although our *maamar* focuses on the condition in which one's love of G-d becomes concealed, in truth, this idea applies to fear of G-d (*yirah*) as well.

To explain: The essential qualities of the soul, which is "truly a part of G-d above," are love and fear of G-d. In its pure and pristine state, the soul is bound up with its root and source in the Creator in a most conscious manner, and is permeated with the highest degree of love and awe natural to it. When it descends into this world and is incorporated in a physical body with material thoughts and desires, the tremendous, glowing love and fear of G-d becomes obscured by the physical surroundings in which the soul finds itself. Consequently, these essential qualities of the soul remain concealed in the heart and mind, in the form of "hidden" love and awe.

14. *Zohar* I:6a; *Tikkunei Zohar,* 5 (19a).

NEKUDA B'HEICHALA: A *nekuda,* a point, has no width or breadth. Similarly, this love of G-d, in its primitive, "hidden" state, lacks expanse—it is but a single "point" of love within the vast "expanse" of the heart.

Nonetheless, this point of love has the potential to eventually blossom into a fully conscious, flaming G-dly ardor, just as a single seedling contains within it all that which will eventually grow from it (the tree trunk, the branches, the leaves, the fruit, etc.).

The problem, the *maamar* explains, is that sometimes man is too submerged within corporeality to tap into this potentially limitless love that lies within his heart. When one does receive a spiritual "wake-up call," however, like on the Shabbat and festivals, one may then realize and experience the full force of this

בְּשֵׁם אֶסְתֵּר. שֶׁהִיא מְסוּתֶּרֶת בִּבְחִינַת בַּיּוֹם הַהוּא שֶׁאֵינָהּ בְּהִתְגַּלּוּת.

וְהִיא בְּחִינַת נְקוּדָה בְּהֵיכָלָא בִּפְנִימִיּוּת נְקוּדַת לִבּוֹ וַדַּאי מְסוּתֶּרֶת הִיא הָאַהֲבָה בְּכָל נֶפֶשׁ מִיִּשְׂרָאֵל וְאֵין לְךְ אָדָם שֶׁאֵין לוֹ בְּחִינַת פְּנִימִיּוּת זוֹ אֶלָּא שֶׁלְּהוֹצִיא מֵהַהֶעְלֵם אֶל הַגִּלּוּי אֵינָהּ שָׁוָה בְּכָל אָדָם.

וְלָכֵן לִימוֹת הַמָּשִׁיחַ שֶׁאָז יְזֻדַּךְ הָאָדָם אֲזַי יִהְיֶה בִּבְחִינַת וְנִגְלָה כְּבוֹד ה' וְרָאוּ כָל בָּשָׂר וגו'. וְאָמַר בַּיּוֹם הַהוּא הִנֵּה אֱלֹהֵינוּ זֶה קִוִּינוּ לוֹ וגו'.

פֵּירוּשׁ שֶׁיָּאִיר אוֹר ה' בְּהִתְגַּלּוּת עַד שֶׁיְּהֵא נִתְפָּס וְנִקְבָּע אֲפִילוּ בְּמוֹחוֹ וְשֵׂכֶל אֱנוֹשִׁי וְרָאוּ כָל בָּשָׂר בִּרְאִיָּה

---

love (see below, Chapter 3).

15. From time to time this subconscious love of G-d does seep into one's consciousness, for even the most wicked of men may suddenly be inspired with true remorse, without prior invocation. This unprovoked inspiration stems solely from one's quintessential love of G-d. (*Maamarei Admur Ha'emtza'ee*, ibid., p. 381.)

16. Depending on the individual, this "point" of love can take on varying forms of expression. In more simple folk, it is expressed as simple refrain from sin, and as pure, self-sacrifice for G-d. In those who are more spiritually advanced, it expresses itself sometimes as a burning, rapturous love of G-d, and sometimes as a feeling of grief and humility. (Ibid.)

17. In the Messianic Age, mankind, to-gether with the entirety of creation, will be raised to a new plane of spiritual sensitivity. Consequently, G-d's radiance will be manifest, for divine revelation is directly correlated with man's refinement.

18. Isaiah 40:5.

19. Ibid. 25:9.

Note the end of *Taanit*: "In the future, the Holy One, blessed be He, will make a circle of the righteous, and He will sit amongst them, in the Garden of Eden. Then, each one will [be able to] point with his finger [to G-d], as it says, "And they will say on that day, 'Behold, *this* is our G-d; we hoped to Him that He would save us.'" The Talmud interprets the phrase, "Behold, this is our G-d," to indicate divine manifestation, an idea our *maamar* will soon mention.

(manifestation) is what "we hoped for"[20]—as opposed to *hu* [which connotes concealment].

3.

HOLY DAYS ... TIMES OF TRANSCENDANCE

Our sages have said that all of the Jewish festivals will be abolished in the Messianic age, save for the holiday of Purim;[21] as the verse declares, "And these days of Purim will never pass from among the Jews, nor shall their memory depart from their descendants."[22] Likewise, our sages maintain that *halachah*, or Jewish Law, will not be abolished in the Future Time.[23]

The meaning of this:

On Shabbat and festivals [there is a colossal shift in creation, in which] all of the worlds—and the sparks of divinity contained therein—transcend their usual standing and are elevated to a "higher" state.[24] Every Jewish soul, being a "spark of divinity," also ex-

---

20. Indeed, it is our yearning and longing throughout the darkness of exile to see G-dliness that is the catalyst for our ultimately experiencing this awesome revelation. (*Maamarei Admur Ha'emtza'ee*, ibid, p. 382.) [This idea mirrors the "crying of Esther"—the catalyst for divine manifestation—as is explained below in Chapter 10.]

21. *Midrash Mishlei* 9:2; *Yalkut Shimoni, Mishlei*, sect. 944.

ABOLISHMENT OF THE FESTIVALS: This is not to be taken literally, for the Torah and its *mitzvot* are immutable. (See *Rambam, Hilchot Yesodei Hatorah* 9:1: "It is clear and explicit in the Torah, that a *mitzvah* from G-d endures forever, without change, addition or diminishment, as the verse states (Deuteronomy 13:1), 'The entire word that I command you, that you shall observe to do; you shall not add to it and you shall not subtract from it.' Likewise, it is written, 'And it is revealed to us and our children forever, to fulfill all the

words of the Torah' (ibid. 29:28). This teaches us that we are obligated to fulfill all the words of the Torah forever, as the verse says, 'An eternal decree for all your generations' (Leviticus 3:17)...." See also *Rambam, Hilchot Melachim* 11:3: "The main point is this: The decrees and laws of this Torah will never change; they will not be added to nor diminished from..."; see also *Kuntres* "*Halachot Shel Torah Shebaal Peh She'enan B'telin L'olam,*" *Sefer Hasichot 5752*, vol. 1, p. 27 ff.).

Rather, the meaning of this *Midrash* is that due to the tremendous divine revelation in the Messianic Era, the spiritual light that shines forth during the festivals will be essentially indiscernible, like the glow of a candle in the daylight. (*Maamarei Admur Ha'emtza'ee*, ibid., p. 396 ff.; *Sefer Hamaamarim 5626*, p. 29. Cf. *Shaalot u'Teshuvot ha'Rashba*, 93; *Chatam Sofer, D'rashot* vol. 1 p. 164a, 196a.)

Thus, the fact that Purim (and *halachah*) will *not* be "abolished" indicates that even in the brilliant radiance of the

גַשְׁמִית חוּשִׁיִּית כִּי אֱלֹהֵינוּ הוּא בְּחִינַת זֶה אֲשֶׁר לָזֶה
קִוִּינוּ לוֹ וְלֹא בִּבְחִינַת הַהוּא:

‏.ג

וְהִנֵּה אָמְרוּ רַבּוֹתֵינוּ זִכְרוֹנָם לִבְרָכָה כָּל הַמּוֹעֲדִים
יִהְיוּ בְּטֵלִים לֶעָתִיד לָבֹא חוּץ מִפּוּרִים שֶׁנֶּאֱמַר וִימֵי
הַפּוּרִים וְגוֹ' וְזִכְרָם לֹא יָסוּף מִזַּרְעָם. וְגַם אָמְרוּ
רַבּוֹתֵינוּ זִכְרוֹנָם לִבְרָכָה הֲלָכוֹת אֵינָן בְּטֵלִים לֶעָתִיד
לָבֹא.

וְהָעִנְיָן הוּא כִּי הִנֵּה עִנְיַן שַׁבָּתוֹת וְיָמִים טוֹבִים הוּא
שֶׁבָּהֶם הוּא בְּחִינַת עֲלִיַּית הָעוֹלָמוֹת וְהַנִּצוֹצוֹת שֶׁכָּל

Future Time, the spiritual light it exudes will be of significance, being of a similar magnitude (as will be explained below in Chapters 7 and 8).

22. Esther 9:28.

23. Jerusalem Talmud, *Megillah* 1:5.

24. ALIYAT HA'OLAMOT: This concept is one that is found often throughout Kabbalistic and Chasidic literature, referring to the state of the worlds on Shabbat and festivals. Obviously, this *aliya* (elevation) is meant to be understood in a strictly spiritual sense, that the worlds become nearer and more receptive to G-d.

As the *maamar* will soon explain, the catalyst of this *aliya* is such: On Shabbat and festivals, each and every world —including ours—is infused with an extra measure of G-dliness. That in turn causes the world to "ascend" and draw nearer to G-d.

Now, this "elevation of the worlds" occurs every Shabbat and festival day, though we may not detect a physical change in the world at those times. This is because our fleshly eye sees only the "surface level" of things, while the *aliya* transformation occurs on the "energy level," a plane indiscernible to our eyes.

To cite an example:

Food normally contains both positive and negative energy. When one eats in order to remain healthy and to aid in one's divine service, one taps into the positive energy of the food, while when one eats merely out of base, animal hunger, one taps into its negative energy. On Shabbat, however, due to the "elevation of the worlds," the negative energy within food dissipates, leaving behind just the positive energy. Thus, even when one eats on Shabbat strictly for pleasure, one is still performing a *mitzvah*, for there are no negative elements left in the food. This holds true though the eye perceives the food to be identical periences this "elevation," caused by an intensification of divine radiance during these times. Thus, on these special days the soul is injected with extra light, joy and spiritual ecstasy, inflaming the soul to cleave to G-d with greater passion than usual.[25]

PASSOVER PASSION

Particularly during the holiday of Passover, the radiance of supernal love, which emanates from divine loving-kindness (*chesed*), shines within every soul. Consequently, every Jewish soul-spark is elevated to a place of spiritual sensitivity, where it is aroused with tremendous love and passion for G-d, and the commitment to completely eradicate any obstacle that might compromise this love: i.e., worldly passions that by their very definition oppose and contradict love of G-d.[26] The process of breaking one's worldly desires is called "*le'achfaya le'sitra achara*"—forcing those negative desires to be under the guide of one's spiritual drive.[27]

DESTROYING THE OPPOSITION

The idea that worldly passions prevent G-dly love, and as such must be destroyed, is demonstrated in the verse, "Who struck Egypt through its firstborn, for His kindness (*chassdo*) is everlasting (*l'olam*)."[28] I.e., in order for the radiance of supernal love (*chesed*) to illuminate the world (*olam*), He smote the firstborn of Egypt, those elements that contradict G-dly love.[29]

[In a similar vein, on every Shabbat and festival there is a manifestation of divine radiance that causes the Jewish people to rise from the grip of materiality and ascend to spiritual heights.[30]]

---

to the food that was eaten throughout the week.

Nonetheless, this *aliya* does have somewhat of an effect on the "surface plane" of our world as well. Indeed, our sages cite examples of the "rest" and sanctity of the Shabbat affecting physical elements—like the Sambatyon River, whose currents come to a rest every Shabbat. (See *Bereishit Rabbah* 11:5.)

For a lengthy explanation of this topic, see *Likkutei Sichot*, vol. 15, p. 55 ff.

25. Moreover, the spiritual charge we receive at these times remains with us throughout the entire year, continuously filling us with extra strength and encouragement in our divine service. (*Maamarei Admur Ha'emtza'ee*, p. 383.)

26. As explained above (footnote 11), one's heart cannot contain love for two contradictory elements.

27. *Zohar* II:129b.

נִצוֹץ נִשְׁמַת יִשְׂרָאֵל מִתְעַלֶּה בְּמַדְרֵגָה מִפְּנֵי אוֹר ה׳
הַמִּתְגַּלֶּה בְּעִתִּים הָהֵם וְנִתּוֹסֵף בָּהֶם אוֹרָה וְשִׂמְחָה
וְחֶדְוַת ה׳ לְהַלְהִיט הַנְּשָׁמוֹת לְדָבְקָה בּוֹ יִתְבָּרֵךְ בְּיֶתֶר
שְׂאֵת

וּבִפְרָטוּת בַּפֶּסַח מִתְגַּלֶּה אוֹר הָאַהֲבָה חֶסֶד עֶלְיוֹן
בִּפְנִימִיּוּת הַנְּשָׁמוֹת. וְעַל יְדֵי זֶה מִתְעַלִּים כָּל נִצוֹצֵי
נִשְׁמוֹת יִשְׂרָאֵל לְעוֹרֵר אֶת הָאַהֲבָה רַבָּה לַה׳ וְלִדְחוֹת
כָּל הַמּוֹנְעִים הַמְבַטְּלִים דְּהַיְינוּ הַדְּבָרִים שֶׁהֵם הֵפֶךְ
וְנֶגֶד אַהֲבַת ה׳ שֶׁהֵם תַּאֲוֹת גַּשְׁמִיִּם לְאַכְפְיָא לְסִטְרָא
אָחֳרָא.

וּכְמוֹ שֶׁכָּתוּב לְמַכֵּה מִצְרַיִם בִּבְכוֹרֵיהֶם כִּי לְעוֹלָם
חַסְדּוֹ. פֵּירוּשׁ שֶׁבִּכְדֵי שֶׁיָּאִיר לְעוֹלָם אוֹר הַחֶסֶד
עֶלְיוֹן הִכָּה בְּכוֹרֵי מִצְרַיִם שֶׁהֵם הֵם הַהֲפָכִים מִזֶּה.

---

28. Psalms 136:10.

29. Chasidut explains that the "Firstborn of Egypt" connotes the *kelipah*, or "negative shell," of Egypt. More specifically, this refers to *kelipah d'chochmah*, a state of perversion of the mind and intellect, where one's thoughts revolve solely around material, narcissistic matters. Eventually, this causes one to completely lose all spiritual awareness, G-d forbid, causing one's mind and heart to become totally insensitive to G-dliness.

30. On each of the three major festivals, one of the three primary *middot* (divine attributes) shines. On Pesach, as the *maamar* explains, *chesed* flows into creation. On Shavuot, G-dly fear and awe (*gevurah*) is manifest in Creation, as it was when the Torah was originally given, amidst "thunder and lightning," arousing in man the desire to reject all of the negative elements that exist in one's character. On Sukkot, divine compassion (*tiferet*) is manifest. (*Maamarei Admur Ha'emtza'ee*, ibid.)

4.

AN UPLIFTING ALLEGORY

[We find this ascent of the Jewish people on Shabbat and festivals alluded to in another verse.] It is written, "Who is this that rises from the wilderness, like columns of smoke, perfumed with myrrh and frankincense, with every powder of the merchant?"[31]

Allegorically, we can expound the verse as follows:

DEPARTING DESOLATION

"Who is this (*zot*) that rises from the wilderness (*midbar*)"

"*Zot*" refers to the Jewish nation,[32] who "rises from the wilderness" of physicality on Shabbat and festivals. "Wilderness" connotes those material elements that are antithetical to G-dliness, elements that are virtually a spiritual wasteland. "Wilderness," or "*midbar*," is also etymologically related to the word "*dibbur*," meaning speech, in this context referring to idle chatter. On Shabbat and festivals, the soul rises from this wasteland.[33]

SMOKE AND FIRE

"Like columns of smoke"

When this spiritual transformation occurs, it is "like columns of smoke." Smoke is produced when fire consumes a conflicting element. For example, when one burns wood or a wick, it is the flame's consumption of the moisture found within the wood and the wick that causes the smoke.[34] Thus, the more moisture contained in any given object, the more smoke that will result when it is burned.

---

31. Song of Songs 3:6. Rashi explains this verse to be speaking of the nations' reaction to Israel's traverse through the desert. They exclaimed: "How great is the spectacle of this nation that is ascending from the wilderness, who journey with a pillar of fire and a cloud clearing the way for them, and a 'cloud of incense' emanating from the Altar…" (For alternative interpretations, see *Targum* and *Metzudat David* on the verse.)

32. Virtually all of the commentaries explain that the subject of this verse ("*zot*") is the Jewish nation. Chasidic thought, however, sheds new light upon this interpretation, explaining the deeper connection between the word *zot* and the Jewish people.

In the holy tongue, both *zeh* and *zot* are translated as "this." The difference lies in their usage: *zeh* is used in a masculine context, while *zot* is used in a feminine context.

Now, before their descent into this world, the souls of Israel rest in the divine

ד.

כְּמוֹ שֶׁכָּתוּב מִי זֹאת עוֹלָה מִן הַמִּדְבָּר כְּתִמְרֹת עָשָׁן
מְקוּטֶּרֶת מוֹר וּלְבוֹנָה מִכֹּל אַבְקַת רוֹכֵל.

פֵּירוּשׁ

כְּנֶסֶת יִשְׂרָאֵל נִקְרֵאת זֹאת הִיא עוֹלָה מִן הַמִּדְבָּר
שֶׁהֵם דְּבָרִים הַגַּשְׁמִיִּים אֲשֶׁר לֹא לַה' הֵמָּה שֶׁהֵם
דּוֹמִים לְמָקוֹם מִדְבָּר וּשְׁמָמָה וְגַם מִדְבָּר מִלְּשׁוֹן דִּבּוּר
דְּהַיְינוּ דְּבָרִים בְּטֵלִים וְהִיא עוֹלָה מֵהֶם בְּשַׁבָּתוֹת
וּמוֹעֲדִים

וְאָז הוּא כְּתִמְרוֹת עָשָׁן כִּי כְּמוֹ שֶׁעָשָׁן גַּשְׁמִי
הִתְהַוּוּתוֹ הוּא מֵחֲמַת שֶׁהָאֵשׁ שׂוֹרֵף דָּבָר שֶׁהוּא הֶפֶךְ
טִבְעוֹ דְּהַיְינוּ לַחְלוּחִית שֶׁיֵּשׁ בָּעֵצִים אוֹ בַּפְּתִילָה שֶׁנֶּאֱחָז
בָּהֶם הָאֵשׁ שֶׁהֲרֵי רִבּוּי הֶעָשָׁן הוּא לְפִי רִבּוּי הַלַּחְלוּחִית
שֶׁיֵּשׁ בַּדָּבָר הַהוּא.

---

sefirah of *malchut* (sovereignty, kingship). *Malchut*, being the last of the ten *sefirot* (see footnote 45), embodies receptivity, for while the other *sefirot* give forth from their light to the *sefirot* below them, *malchut* merely contains that which it receives from above.

Thus, the term *zot* (femininity, receptivity) used in our verse alludes to the souls who are rooted in *malchut* (receptivity). [It is for this same reason that Israel is sometimes alluded to with the term *isha*, or woman, as we will see in Chapter 6. See also footnote 77.]

33. In the concluding statements of *Kuntres Acharon*, Rabbi Schneur Zalman writes: "Be most careful not to indulge in idle chatter [on Shabbat], G-d forbid, for ... the deeper meaning of 'Observe [the Shabbat]' is refraining from speaking about material affairs."

34. Every physical entity is comprised of four fundamental elements: fire, water, air and earth. (See *True Existence*, Kehot, p. 43 ff.) Collectively, these elements are the "building blocks" of virtually all matter. Though an object may appear to be comprised of only one or two of these elements, it, in reality, is a composite of all four. Thus, even a "dry" object such as wood naturally contains some moisture—the element of water.

Similarly, on the Shabbat and festivals, when the divine radiance is manifest, it "burns" and "consumes" (so to speak) those elements that oppose G-dliness, "*le'achfaya le'sitra achara,*" thereby producing spiritual "smoke."

G-D IS IN THE DETAILS
"Perfumed"

"Perfume" is called "thin smoke," like "the smoke of incense."[35] Because of its fine nature, the Torah refers to incense not as smoke but as a cloud, as it says, "so that the *cloud* of the incense shall blanket…"[36] The reason why burning incense produces relatively thin smoke is because the fire does not need to consume an element that is diametrically opposed to itself; within the incense are elements that are only *somewhat* resistant to the flame.

Nevertheless, there must be, at this point, the idea of "perfume"—to burn and consume [even the most subtle of negative traits] from [within] every individual, in accordance with one's personal level and the value of his soul, as he progresses spiritually.[37]

RETROSPECTION
"With myrrh"

This is similar to the verse in the *Megillah*, "Now when each maiden's turn came to go to King Ahasuerus [after … six months with *oil of myrrh*…]."[38]

Every Jewish soul-spark is as a "maiden" before G-d, which yearns to "come to the King," to ascend and perceive the divine radiance, each soul on its particular level.

"Six months with oil of myrrh." Oil represents *chochmah,* wisdom.[39] Myrrh is etymologically related to the word *merirut,*

---

35. See *Shabbat* 18a, and Rashi's commentary.

36. Leviticus 16:13.

37. Even after one has destroyed one's sinful lusts, one may still possess desire for those things that are permitted by the Torah. These elements, though permissible, nonetheless keep man fettered to materiality, and thus limit the scope of one's spiritual experience. Therefore, our sages say (*Yevamot* 20a), "Sanctify yourself with that which is permitted to you." (*Or Hatorah, Megillat Esther,* p. 119.)

38. Esther 2:12.

39. OIL AND CHOCHMAH. See *Menachot* 85b: "Tekoa was the leading city in

כָּךְ כִּבְיָכוֹל כְּשֶׁאוֹר ה' מִתְגַּלֶּה בְּשַׁבָּתוֹת וְיָמִים טוֹבִים שׂוֹרֵף וּמְכַלֶּה דְּבַר הַהֵפוּךְ הַגָּלוּי לְאַכְפָיְיא לְסִטְרָא אָחֳרָא.

וְגַם הִיא מְקוּטֶּרֶת קִיטוֹר נִקְרָא עָשָׁן דַּק כְּמוֹ עֶשֶׁן הַמֻּגְמָר וְהַקְּטוֹרֶת וּלְרוֹב דַּקּוּתוֹ לֹא נִקְרָא בַּתּוֹרָה בְּשֵׁם עָשָׁן כִּי אִם בְּשֵׁם עָנָן כְּמוֹ שֶׁכָּתוּב וְכִסָּה עֲנַן הַקְּטוֹרֶת. וְהַיְינוּ מִפְּנֵי שֶׁאֵינוּ שׂוֹרֵף וּמְכַלֶּה דְּבַר הַהֵפוּךְ מַמָּשׁ לְפִי שֶׁאֵין בַּדָּבָר הַנֶּאֱחָז בָּהֶם הָאוֹר מִדְּבַר הַהֵפֶךְ כִּי אִם מְעַט מִזְעֵיר

וְאַף עַל פִּי כֵן צְרִיכָה לִהְיוֹת בִּבְחִינָה זוֹ בִּבְחִינַת מְקוּטֶּרֶת לְשָׂרוּף וּלְכַלּוֹת כָּל אֶחָד לְפִי מַדְרֵגָתוֹ וּלְפִי מַעֲלַת נִשְׁמָתוֹ בְּעִילּוּי אַחַר עִילּוּי

וְאַחַר כָּךְ יִהְיֶה בִּבְחִינַת מוֹר הוּא הָאָמוּר בַּמְּגִילָה בְּהַגִּיעַ תּוֹר נַעֲרָה וְנַעֲרָה לָבֹא אֶל הַמֶּלֶךְ

שֶׁכָּל נִצוֹץ יִשְׂרָאֵל הֵם בִּבְחִינַת נוּקְבָא לְגַבֵּי הַקָּדוֹשׁ בָּרוּךְ הוּא לַעֲלוֹת וְלִרְאוֹת בְּאוֹר ה' כָּל אֶחָד לְפִי מַדְרֵגָתוֹ

שִׁשָּׁה חֳדָשִׁים בְּשֶׁמֶן הַמֹּר שֶׁמֶן הַמֹּר הוּא בְּחִינַת חָכְמָה

Israel for oil [to use in the *Beit Ha-mikdash*]. [In II Samuel 4:2, we are told that] 'Joab sent to Tekoa and brought a wise woman from there' [in order to convince King David to reconcile with Absalom]. Why did he specifically choose a woman from Tekoa? Rabbi Yochanan said: Since they were accustomed to [partaking of] olive oil, they were wise." As

Rashi explains, "Olive oil opens the heart."

Kabblistic and Chasidic texts note several similarities between oil and *chochmah*:
1. Oil can be extracted from every form of matter: animal, vegetable and mineral. Similarly, the essential quality of *chochmah*—*bittul* (self-abnegation)—is found within all of creation, for "You

bitterness.[40] Thus, [the *Megillah* is saying that] after one has climbed out of his spiritual "wasteland" and has crushed and separated the negative elements, thereby enabling them to be consumed and burned as "smoke" and "incense," one can then truly understand and appreciate how "bitter" these elements truly are.[41]

HAPPY HORIZONS

"And frankincense"

After one has gone through this spiritual transformation and recognizes the bitterness of the past, one can then bask in the joy of spiritual ecstasy:[42] "Israel will rejoice in its Maker."[43]

This is alluded to in the continuation of the verse in the *Megillah*: "And six months with perfumes…"[44]

Perfume presents us with an interesting paradox. Although its scent is intangible and is indiscernible to the eye, it nonetheless causes the person pleasure and satisfaction when it seeps into the body.

---

have made them all with *chochmah*."

2. A single drop of oil extracted from any given substance will contain its essential qualities, just as *chochmah*, the initial "flash" of intellectual conception, contains the "essence," the entire "width" and "breadth," of the idea.

3. Oil is extracted (from many elements) through pressing and crushing, a process analogous to the concept of *bittul* reflected in *chochmah*.

4. When mixed with other liquids, oil invariably floats to the top. *Chochmah*, too, is the first of the ten *sefirot* and is considered to be well "removed" from the other nine. In the words of *Tanya* (Chapter 35, in gloss), "The light of the Infinite One, blessed be He, does not become unified even in the world of *Atzilut*, unless it clothes itself first in the *sefirah* of *chochmah*. This is because the Infinite One, blessed be He, is the True One, Who is One Alone, and apart from Whom there is nothing—and this is the level of *chochmah*…"

(*Torah Or* 39a, 40d, 81c; *Maamarei*

Admur Hazaken 5568, vol. 2, p. 647; *Sefer Halikkutim, Shemen*. See also *Shaar Hayichud v'HaEmunah*, chapter 9.)

40. MERIRUT (AND ATZVUT). Chasidut differentiates between two types of sorrow: *merirut* (lit. bitterness), a constructive grief, and *atzvut* (depression), a destructive grief.

The first is the distress of one who not only recognizes his failings but also cares about them; one who agonizes over the wrongs he has committed, over his missed opportunities, over his unrealized potential; one who refuses to become indifferent to what is deficient in himself and his world. The second is the distress of one who has despaired of himself and his fellow man, whose melancholy has drained him of hope and initiative. The first is a springboard for self-improvement; the second, a bottomless pit.

Merirut, then, is a healthy, necessary ingredient in one's divine service, a crucial part of the introspective process, while *atzvut* is a stepping-stone to disaster, a

לִהְיוֹת בִּבְחִינַת מוֹר בִּבְחִינַת מְרִירוּת שֶׁמֵּאַחַר שֶׁעוֹלָה
מִן הַמִּדְבָּר וּמְפָרֵר וּמַפְרִיד הָרָע לִהְיוֹת כָּלֶה וְנִשְׂרָף
בְּעָשָׁן וְקִיטוֹר אֲזַי יַשְׂכִּיל הֵיטֵב עִנְיַן הַמְּרִירוּת מִן הַהֵפֶךְ
אֵיךְ וּמָה הוּא

וְאַחַר כַּךְ יָבֹא לִבְחִינַת לְבוֹנָה הִיא בְּחִינַת הַשִּׂמְחָה
בְּחֶדְוַת ה' יִשְׂמַח יִשְׂרָאֵל בְּעוֹשָׂיו:

וְזֶהוּ עִנְיַן שִׁשָּׁה חֲדָשִׁים בַּבְּשָׂמִים

כִּי כְּמוֹ שֶׁהָרֵיחַ נִקְלָט וְנִכְנָס לְתוֹךְ גּוּפוֹ וּמְעַנֵּג בַּדֶּשֶׁן
נַפְשׁוֹ הֲגַם שֶׁהוּא דָּבָר שֶׁאֵין בּוֹ מַמָּשׁ וְאֵין נִרְאֶה
וְנִתְגַּלֶּה לָעַיִן רַק נִקְלָט הָרֵיחַ לְתוֹךְ גּוּפוֹ.

---

dangerous, destructive trap that must be avoided at all costs.

41. While one retains desire for physical things, one cannot feel that these elements are truly bitter, for he is still attached to them. Only after one eradicates even the minutest material desire, freeing himself of all physical drives, can one truly experience grief.

42. Rabbi DovBer writes in his aforementioned *maamar*: "Frankincense, which includes all types of fragrant perfumes, stems from [the *sefirah* of] *binah*, the level of G-dly joy and delight." (It is worth noting that the Hebrew word for frankincense, *le'vonah*, is closely related to the word *binah*.)

Why does *binah* represent "joy and delight"?

Binah, in human terms, is the intellectual stage of comprehension, where an idea that existed previously as a mere conceptual "flash" (*chochmah*) is now fully developed in one's mind. It is at this stage,

when the individual has chewed through a thought and finally understands it fully, that he may experience pleasure from his intellectual triumph. Indeed, the very fact that something previously hidden is now revealed to him excites him greatly.

The same applies to the supernal *sefirah* of *binah*, the realm of G-dly comprehension, where divinity is understood in all of its "width" and "breadth." It is precisely in *binah*, the *sefirah* of understanding, where "G-dly joy and delight" reside.

[Hence the verse (Psalms 113:9), "A joyful mother of children": "Mother of children" refers to *binah*, the *sefirah* that yields emotional "progeny." (One's intellectual comprehension invariably produces feelings of emotion.) Thus, it is the "mother of children," *binah*, that is "joyful."] (*Likuttei Torah, D'rushim L'Sukkot,* 79d; *Sefer Hamaamarim 5654*, p. 21.)

43. Psalms 149:2.

44. Esther ibid.

The same is true regarding one's spiritual joy. Although this delight stems from a realm that lies beyond our comprehension, a realm that to us is "hidden" and indiscernible (*alma d'itkasya*),[45] nonetheless, it inflames one's very heart with divine passion and joy to bask in G-dly radiance.

SPIRITUAL POTPOURRI
"With every powder of the merchant"
This refers to the many different kinds of spiritual passion that can be ignited in one's soul, for the degree of passion is dependant upon one's particular spiritual standing. This is also the same idea as "the feminine cosmetics" [mentioned at the conclusion of the verse in the *Megillah*]: with all of these cosmetics [i.e. the various G-dly passions experienced by each soul], the "maiden" (soul) "comes before the King" (G-d).[46]

5.

REALITY CHECK
Now, all forms of the elevation and drawing close of the Jewish

---

45. ALMA D'ITKASYA: Lit., "the hidden realm." Man is comprised of ten *kochot hanefesh*, or "soul-powers," ten distinct intellectual and emotional faculties that operate in man's consciousness. They are, briefly: *chochmah* (wisdom, conception), *binah* (understanding, comprehension), *da'at* (knowledge, focus), *chesed* (kindness, grace), *gevurah* (severity, might), *tiferet* (beauty, harmony), *netzach* (endurance, victory), *hod* (splendor, majesty), *yesod* (foundation, connection) and *malchut* (sovereignty, kingship).

More specifically, these ten *kochot* are divided into two categories: the first three are intellectual "powers," termed *sechel*, while the remaining seven are emotional "powers," called *middot*.

The natures of *sechel* and *middot* differ greatly. The faculties of *sechel* can be used by man in solitary study, to analyze, decipher and ultimately understand any given topic, *alone*. They thus fall within the more "introverted" domain of man. *Middot*, conversely, can only function in relation to someone or something apart from oneself. One can only exercise kindness or severity on another; it is illogical to say that one is implementing kindness on *oneself*. *Middot* thus represent man's capacity for "extroversion."

Everything that exists in man has its spiritual, cosmic counterpart. Indeed, it is from this metaphysical place that man's characteristics are born. Thus, there exist ten identical supernal "faculties," known as the ten *sefirot*, which serve as the origin of their more terrestrial forms. And they, too, are comprised of the two categories, *sechel* and *middot*.

The same characteristics that define human *sechel* and *middot* also mark their

כָּךְ עִנְיָן הַשִּׂמְחָה בַּה' הוּא מֵעָלְמָא דְאִתְכַּסְיָא רַק
שֶׁמְּשַׂמַּחַת אֶת הַלֵּב וּמַלְהִיטוֹ לְהִתְלַהֵט וּלְהִתְלַהֵב בְּאוֹר ה'

מִכֹּל אַבְקַת רוֹכֵל הֵם כָּל מִינֵי הִתְלַהֲבוּת אֲשֶׁר
בְּכָל נֶפֶשׁ מִיִּשְׂרָאֵל כָּל חַד לְפוּם שִׁעוּרָא דִילֵיהּ. וְהוּא
עִנְיָן בְּתַמְרוּקֵי הַנָּשִׁים שֶׁבְּכָל אֵלּוּ הַנַּעֲרָה בָּאָה אֶל
הַמֶּלֶךְ:

ה.

וְהִנֵּה כָּל מִינֵי עֲלִיּוֹת וְהִתְקָרְבוּת כְּנֶסֶת יִשְׂרָאֵל

---

supernal complement. Divine s*echel* are the attributes that are focused solely internally, on G-d, while divine *middot* are the attributes that relate to beings "outside" of G-d.

Thus, in Kabbalistic texts the *middot* are called *alma d'itgalya*, "the revealed realms," for since they can relate to our existence, they are considered to be "revealed" to us. *Sechel*, on the other hand, and particularly *binah*, is termed *alma d'itkasya*, "the hidden realm," since it is totally removed and "hidden" from all of creation, being focused solely on G-d.

Therefore, one's spiritual joy, which stems from the *sefirah* of *binah* (as explained in footnote 42), is considered to be from *alma d'itkasya*, "the hidden realm," since as part of *sechel* it is beyond existence and "hidden" from it.

[Although we explained before that *binah* represents "revelation," as in a newfound comprehension of a previously unknown concept, that is as *binah* relates to the thinker himself. To him, *binah* spells revelation and joy. For someone else, however, *binah* epitomizes conceal-ment, for at that point the idea exists solely within the mind of the thinker. Likewise with the supernal *sefirah* of *binah*: as it exists within the framework of the *sefirot*, it embodies revelation. As it relates to the created worlds, however, it bespeaks concealment.]

For a more thorough examination of the topic, see the sources cited in footnote 42.

46. Yet, Esther "requested nothing" of the "oil of myrrh," the "perfumes" and the "feminine cosmetics," for these represent varying degrees of divine revelation that the soul may experience during its spiritual ascent, whereas "Esther" refers to the passionate desire found within the quintessence of the soul to connect with G-d Himself, a desire that cannot be sated by perceiving a mere manifestation of G-dliness. (*Maamarei Admur Ha'emtza'ee*, ibid, p. 389.) [The difference between G-d Himself (*Atzmut*) and G-dly manifestation (*giluyim*) will be explained at length in Chapter 5.]

people to the Holy One, blessed be He, on Shabbat and festivals, and every ascent level after level until the most supernal heights—is termed "touching the *tip* of the scepter."

SCEPTER SYMBOLISM

To explain:

The "golden scepter" symbolizes the transmission of divine energy that vivifies all of creation, from the highest realms to the lowest worlds, as is written, "the golden scepter, that he may live."[47] It is therefore impossible for the soul to receive life from the entire "scepter," for the spiritual "light" would prove to be too intense. Rather, the soul can merely accept an emanation from the "tip of the scepter," with the actual scepter remaining in the King's hand.

In the soul, this "emanation" expresses itself as an intense, burning love of G-d, like a flame surging upward; it is therefore called the "higher gold," the "gold of the offering-up."[48]

TWO PATHS TO LOVING G-D

This love is aroused to a lesser degree through meditating upon G-d's infinite greatness, as He both "fills" the worlds (*memalei kol almin*) and "transcends" them (*soveiv kol almin*),[49] the divinity that is

---

47. A homiletic translation of Esther 4:11: "All the king's servant's and all the people of the king's provinces know that any man or woman who goes to the king and enters the inner courtyard without being summoned, his is but one verdict—execution; except for the person to whom the king extends his golden scepter—[only] he shall live."

In a physical sense, the king's golden scepter represented life itself—one standing before the king would be granted life by receiving the scepter. Similarly, in a spiritual sense, the golden scepter represents the supernal transmission of life from the Supreme King, G-d.

48. Exodus 38:24.

GOLD—BURNING LOVE OF G-D: In

Chasidic texts, gold is understood to represent *gevurah* (severity) and fire. ("Gold glitters like… glowing embers"—*Torah Or* 35a.) Thus, the type of love intimated by the "*golden* scepter" is a fiery, flaming, burning love of G-d.

To explain: Typically, love is an expression of *chesed*, kindness. Nonetheless, there is a form of love that stems from *gevurah*, severity, and is likened to a flame. Just as a flame constantly flickers upward, licking the air above while it struggles to break free of the wick's hold, this love too is of a similar nature, one that triggers a desire within man to rise upward and break free of his physical shackles, so that he may be united with G-d. This love, as the *maamar* says, is called the "higher gold" and the "gold of the offering-up,"

לְהַקָּדוֹשׁ בָּרוּךְ הוּא בְּשַׁבָּת וְיוֹם טוֹב וְכָל מַה שֶּׁמִּתְעַלּוֹת
בְּעִילּוּי אַחַר עִילּוּי עַד רוּם הַמַּעֲלוֹת נִקְרָאִים בְּשֵׁם נְגִיעָה
בְּרֹאשׁ הַשַּׁרְבִיט

כִּי שַׁרְבִיט הַזָּהָב הוּא הַמְשָׁכַת אוֹר אֵין סוֹף בָּרוּךְ
הוּא וְהוּא הוּא חַיּוּת כָּל הָעוֹלָמוֹת עֶלְיוֹנִים וְתַחְתּוֹנִים
כְּמוֹ שֶׁכָּתוּב אֶת שַׁרְבִיט הַזָּהָב וְחָיָה וְאֵינָהּ יְכוֹלָה
לַעֲלוֹת וְלִרְאוֹת וּלְקַבֵּל חַיּוּתָהּ מִכָּל הַשַּׁרְבִיט. רַק
הַשַּׁרְבִיט נִשְׁאָר בְּיָדוֹ וְרַק הָאָרָה מַגִּיעַ אֵלֶיהָ בְּרֹאשׁ
הַשַּׁרְבִיט

וְהָאָרָה זוֹ הִיא בְּחִינַת אַהֲבָה עַזָּה כְּרִשְׁפֵּי אֵשׁ
וְשַׁלְהֶבֶת הָעוֹלָה לְמַעְלָה זָהָב הָעֶלְיוֹן זָהָב הַתְּנוּפָה

וְקָצֵהוּ הַתַּחְתּוֹן הוּא כְּשֶׁאַהֲבָה עַזָּה זוֹ בּוֹעֲרָה
וּמִתְלַהֶבֶת מֵהִתְבּוֹנְנוּתוֹ בִּגְדוּלַת אֵין סוֹף בָּרוּךְ הוּא

---

for its nature is to cause man to rise "higher" and "offer up" himself to G-d.

[The love discussed by our *maamar* is
the kind that is likened to a flaming fire.
Chasidut also discusses another kind of
G-dly love, one that is likened to water.
The difference between these two loves
can be understood by analyzing the elements of fire and water.

Water is a binding agent. Similarly,
the love that is "like water" is one that fills
man with the desire to be "bound" as one
with G-d; although man retains a feeling
of "self," he wants to connect with G-d.

The nature of fire, on the other hand,
is to consume. Thus, the love that is "like
fire" is one that so utterly consumes man
that he loses all feeling of "self" and existence, being completely suffused in

G-dliness.]

The *maamar* now proceeds to describe
two manners by which the "golden scepter" (burning love of G-d) may be transmitted: either through touching the tip of
the scepter, merely coming in contact
with the bottom end of the scepter, or
through receiving the entire scepter,
touching even its uppermost portion.

49. MEMALEI—SOVEV (IMMANENCE
—TRANSCENDENCE): *Memalei kol almin*
and *soveiv kol almin* are two distinct manners by which divine energy is transmitted
to creation. *Memalei* refers to the divine
energy invested *within* creation, while *soveiv* refers to the divine energy that *transcends* creation.

Memalei kol almin is immanent divine

termed *the bottom of the scepter.*[50]

The most intense measure of divine passion, however, is aroused by meditating upon the "Essence" of G-d Himself (*Atzmut*), *the top of the scepter.* The "Essence" of G-d is to what the dictum "no mind can grasp Him at all"[51] refers. Such terms as "greatness," "immanence" and "transcendence," can only be used when discussing the emanation of divine energy that animates creation. [*Atzmut*, however, which is completely beyond creation, cannot be so labeled.[52]]

ESSENCE AND EMANATION

This idea is expressed in the verse, "[G-d (*Havaya*[53]) is great and exceedingly exalted,] and His greatness is beyond any investigation."[54]

---

energy, measured and limited in accordance with that which is being animated. Since it is limited, it permeates all of creation and is mutually interactive and inter-responsive with the subject that it enlivens. By way of analogy, the life force from the soul is clothed within the body in a way that alters the body fundamentally. It is not simply life-force which enlivens the body; it is the life force *of the body*, that which transforms a dead corpse into a live body.

Soveiv kol almin, on the other hand, acts in a remote, imperative, unidirectional manner (i.e. solely from above to below, but not vice versa).

An analogy: Sunlight shines into a room and illuminates it. However, the room itself is not changed thereby, since the light emanates from a source outside of the room; it is not the room itself that lights up. Even when the light illuminates the room, the walls of the room do not actually absorb the light. The light is merely there as light—an illumination from the luminary—but does not become part of that which it illuminates. Similarly, the energy of *soveiv* is of an infinite order that cannot be confined within limited creatures. It thus "encompasses" them in both a pervasive and transcending form. This is why it is called *makif*: it is "there," but remains remote from that which it animates. (See *Tanya*, chapters 46 and 48; *Sefer HaMaamarim 5703*, p. 31.)

50. As explained above, the extension of the golden scepter is an allegory of the transmission of divine energy that animates creation. Thus, the *bottom of the scepter*, the part that is normally transmitted to one who is standing before the king, alludes to those aspects of divinity that are comprehensible to man, namely, the way G-d is *memalei kol almin* (immanent) and *soveiv kol almin* (transcendent). The *top of the scepter*, in contrast, is never extended to another but remains forever in the king's hand, thus alluding to divinity that is completely removed from creation and beyond all comprehension, that which cannot even be termed *transcendent* (for "transcendence" indicates that there is a relationship, albeit a distant one)—namely, *Atzmut*, G-d's pure, true Essence.

When one meditates upon *the bottom*

מְמַלֵּא כָּל עָלְמִין וְסוֹבֵב כָּל עָלְמִין

וְקָצֵהוּ הָעֶלְיוֹן הוּא כְּשֶׁמִּתְלַהֶבֶת וּמִתְלַהֶטֶת
מֵהִתְבּוֹנְנוּתוֹ בְּמַהוּתוֹ וְעַצְמוּתוֹ יִתְבָּרֵךְ וְלֵית מַחֲשָׁבָה
תְּפִיסָא בֵיהּ כְּלָל וְלֹא שַׁיָּיךְ בֵּיהּ לְשׁוֹן גְּדוּלָה מְמַלֵּא כָּל
עָלְמִין וְסוֹבֵב כָּל עָלְמִין רַק עַל הָאָרֶץ וְהַמְשָׁכַת הַחַיּוּת
מִמֶּנּוּ יִתְבָּרֵךְ שַׁיָּיךְ לוֹמַר מְמַלֵּא וְסוֹבֵב

אֲבָל לִגְדוּלָתוֹ דַּוְקָא אֵין חֵקֶר. פֵּירוּשׁ דְּלֹא שַׁיָּיךְ
כְּלָל לַחֲקוֹר וּלְהִתְבּוֹנֵן בִּגְדוּלָתוֹ אֵיךְ הוּא גָּדוֹל מְאֹד

---

of the scepter, one will be inflamed with divine ardor. But this cannot compare to the love that stems from meditating upon *the top of the scepter*, a love of G-d that is literally boundless in its passion.

51. Introduction to *Tikkunei Zohar* (17a). It is not just that we cannot understand *Atzmut*, but rather that *Atzmut* cannot be understood: i.e., by definition, G-d's Essence is beyond logic and rationale, beyond the entire realm of intellect.

In this vein, *Tanya* states: "It is not at all proper to say concerning the Holy One, blessed be He, Who transcends all intellect and wisdom, that it is impossible to comprehend Him because of the depth of the concept, for He is not within the realm of comprehension at all.

"And one who states that it is not possible to comprehend Him, is as one who says concerning some lofty and profound wisdom that it cannot be touched with the hands because of the depth of the concept, for whoever hears it will mock him because the sense of touch refers and applies to physical objects that may be grasped by the hands. Exactly so, the

quality of intellect and comprehension in relation to the Holy One, blessed be He, is considered as actual physical action." (*Shaar Hayichud v'HaEmunah*, Chapter 9.)

52. ATZMUT: As mentioned earlier, both *memalei kol almin* and *soveiv kol almin* are transmissions of divinity to creation (the only difference being the manner in which they interact with creation). Thus, the Essence of G-d, to which there *is no creation*, cannot be termed *soveiv*, transcendent, for it has absolutely no relationship with the worlds, not even in a "removed" manner.

Similarly, *Atzmut* cannot be termed "great." "Greatness" is an evaluation, a label applied to something that can be understood and therefore measured against something of lesser stature. G-d Himself, however, cannot be understood; thus, He can neither be "measured" nor deemed "great."

53. This is the colloquial form of the ineffable Tetragrammaton, *Y-H-V-H*.

54. Psalms 145:3.

This means that it is only possible to "investigate" and meditate upon the greatness of *Havaya*, the divine energy that is *transmitted to creation*.[55] The "*Essence*" of G-d, however, cannot be investigated and deemed "great," for "all before Him is as nothing,"[56] and to Him it is as if there are no worlds at all.[57]

G-D'S IMMUTABILITY

Thus, scripture states: "I, G-d, have not changed."[58] And, like the Sages proclaim: "You were the same before the world was created; You are the same after the world was created"[59]—equally, without change. For G-d neither "fills" nor "transcends" the worlds: His "Essence" is beyond the realm of the worlds.[60]

---

55. See *Tanya, Shaar Hayichud ve-Ha'Emunah* (beg. chapter 4): "The meaning of the name *Havaya* is, 'That which brings everything into existence *ex nihilo*.'"

56. Paraphrase of Daniel 4:32. See *Zohar* I:11b.

57. The creation of the worlds—and the transmission of life to these worlds—is from a mere reflection of G-d's infinite light (in the form of *memalei kol almin* and *soveiv kol almin*, as explained above). G-d Himself, however, remains distant and removed from the worlds, even after their creation. Thus, to *Atzmut*, it is as if the worlds do not exist.

This will be better understood through an analogy of a father who has small children who play childish games. Although the father is a grown man who cares for more intellectual pursuits, and as such does not have any interest in these simple games, still, out of his great love for his children, he will join in their game if they ask him to. Moreover, he will throw himself entirely into the game, to the point where he is acting exactly like his young progeny.

When the game ends and the father returns to his room to resume his studies, he completely forgets about the whole episode, for to a man of his intellect this was but a childish game—something that does not occupy his thoughts after it is finished. In fact, the only reason that he joined in the game to begin with was out of his love for his children, for whom he would "lower" himself down and get involved with immature, silly games.

Thus, while the father is playing with his children, he is completely involved with the game, to the extent that he expresses joy when he wins and sadness when defeated. When the game is finished, however, all of this is forgotten, for he is really beyond such simple games.

Understanding this example, we can better appreciate the relationship between our Father in Heaven and creation. The entire "realm of creation" exists only as G-d lowers Himself to become involved with creating and sustaining the worlds. G-d Himself, however, is totally beyond all of this, and to Him there is no "realm of creation" at all.

Still, the analogy is not completely accurate, for mortal man cannot exist in two

וּמְהוּלָל אֶלָּא בְּשֵׁם הוי' בָּרוּךְ הוּא הַמּוֹרֶה עַל הַמְשָׁכַת
הַחַיּוּת לָעוֹלָמוֹת. אֲבָל קַמֵּיהּ מַמָּשׁ כְּלָא מַמָּשׁ חֲשִׁיבוּ
וּכְאִלּוּ אֵין שָׁם עוֹלָמוֹת כְּלָל

כְּמוֹ שֶׁכָּתוּב אֲנִי ה' לֹא שָׁנִיתִי וְאַתָּה הוּא קוֹדֶם
שֶׁנִּבְרָא וְאַתָּה הוּא אַחַר שֶׁנִּבְרָא הָעוֹלָם הַכֹּל בְּשָׁוֶה וְלֹא
שַׁיָּיךְ לְפָנָיו יִתְבָּרֵךְ בְּחִינַת עָלְמִין לֹא בִּבְחִינַת מְמַלֵּא וְלֹא
בִּבְחִינַת סוֹבֵב כִּי אֵינוֹ בִּגְדֶר עָלְמִין כְּלָל.

---

opposing states simultaneously. Thus, when the father "lowers himself down" to play with his children, he has at that point left the "realm of wisdom" and cannot think about profound intellectual concepts, for he is then completely invested in the game.

Not so regarding G-d, with Whom two contradictory states can exist simultaneously. Even after He has "lowered Himself down" to reflect a divine light capable of creating and sustaining the worlds, He still remains in His Essential, infinite state, not being limited or held down to the "lower" state from where creation emanates. Thus, at the very same moment G-d invests Himself (so to speak) in creation, there also exists the idea that to G-d's Essence, the worlds have no existence.

On the other hand, however, the *tzimtzum*—the process by which G-d withdraws Himself to allow for the existence of the worlds—is a completely true concept. Thus, the existence of the worlds is not a mere illusion, G-d forbid, but a concrete fact. As the *maamar* precisely states, to G-d Himself "it is *as if* there are no worlds at all," meaning, that although in reality they do exist, still,

since they have no importance to G-d's Essence, it is *as if* they do not exist.

58. Malachi 3:6.

59. Liturgy, Morning Prayer.

60. Since G-d is essentially beyond creation, He is therefore not "invested" in it or affected by it, just as the sun—being "removed" from the rays that issue forth from it—is not affected in the slightest whether the full strength of its rays reaches earth or if there are clouds blocking their path.

[Likewise, in the analogy mentioned above (footnote 57), when the father returns to his room after he has finished playing with his children and resumes his studies, his studies remain completely unaffected by his previous activities, since to him it is as if the game ceases to exist.]

In the words of *Tanya* (Chapter 20): "Just as He was all alone, single and unique, before [the worlds] were created, so is He one and alone, single and unique after they were created, since beside Him, everything is as nothing, literally null and void."

IS 'GREATNESS' GREAT?

It is also written, "The L-rd is great and exceedingly praised, in the city of *Elokeinu*..."[61] And, our Sages explain:[62] "When is He heralded as being "great"? When He is found 'in the city of *Elokeinu*'" [i.e., when speaking of the emanation of divine energy that flows into creation].[63] When referring to G-d Himself, [however,] one cannot use the term "great," for all of creation, from the most supernal of realms to the lowliest worlds, is as nothing to Him.

SUPERNAL SITTING

His "greatness," therefore, is truly His humility,[64] for He [descends and] garbs Himself within "greatness," so that "[His] kingdom [be] the kingdom over all worlds,"[65] as the verse says, "The L-rd will sit as the King *le'olam* (of the world)."[66]

This is what is also is meant by the verse, "And You, holy One (*kadosh*), are enthroned upon the praises of Israel":[67] There can only be "praises of Israel" once G-d has humbled and lowered Himself to be "enthroned" as King of creation.[68] Truthfully, You are *kadosh*, completely removed and beyond creation.[69]

6.

MOSHIACH'S MANIFESTATION...

When Moshiach comes, however, G-d's [*true*] radiance will shine with awesome and brilliant power. I.e., G-d's Essence will flow from

---

61. Psalms 48:2.

62. *Zohar* II:235a; III:5a; *Zohar Chadash, Tisa* 44a; *Chukat* 51d.

63. Each of G-d's seven ineffable names refers to another aspect or attribute of G-dliness.

As mentioned earlier (footnote 55), *Y-H-V-H* refers to the transmission of divine energy that essentially *creates* the worlds. The name *Elokim*, on the other hand, refers to the manner by which G-dliness is *concealed* within creation and nature. [Thus, the numerical value of *Elokim* is equal to *hateva*, nature.] This name is the source of plurality (as it is the only name of G-d with an "—*im*" suffix, indicating the plural form) and limited existence. Thus, City of *Elokeinu* signifies the divine energy that is found and concealed *within* the physical creation.

64. *Megillah* 31a, according to the tex-

וּכְדִכְתִיב גָּדוֹל ה' וּמְהוּלָל מְאֹד בְּעִיר אֱלֹקֵינוּ הַר
קָדְשׁוֹ. וְאָמְרוּ רַבּוֹתֵינוּ זִכְרוֹנָם לִבְרָכָה אֵימָתַי נִקְרָא
גָּדוֹל כְּשֶׁהוּא בְּעִיר אֱלֹקֵינוּ וכו'. כִּי לְפָנָיו יִתְבָּרֵךְ לֹא
שַׁיָּיךְ לְשׁוֹן גְּדוּלָה מֵאַחַר שֶׁכָּל עוֹלָמוֹת עֶלְיוֹנִים
וְתַחְתּוֹנִים כּוּלָּא כְּלָא חֲשִׁיב קַמֵּיהּ

אֶלָּא מִדַּת גְּדוּלָתוֹ הוּא עַנְוְתָנוּתוֹ שֶׁמִּתְלַבֵּשׁ בִּבְחִינַת
גְּדוּלָה כְּדֵי לִהְיוֹת מַלְכוּתוֹ מַלְכוּת כָּל עוֹלָמִים. וּכְמוֹ
שֶׁכָּתוּב וַיֵּשֶׁב ה' מֶלֶךְ לְעוֹלָם.

וְזֶהוּ וְאַתָּה קָדוֹשׁ יוֹשֵׁב תְּהִלּוֹת יִשְׂרָאֵל. פֵּירוּשׁ
שֶׁלִּהְיוֹתְךָ תְּהִלּוֹת יִשְׂרָאֵל הוּא בְּחִינַת יְשִׁיבָה שֶׁהוּא
הַשְׁפָּלָה וַעֲנָוָה אֶצְלְךָ שֶׁבֶּאֱמֶת אַתָּה קָדוֹשׁ וּמוּבְדָּל מִגֶּדֶר זֶה.

ו.

אֲבָל לֶעָתִיד יִתְגַּלֶּה אוֹר ה' בְּגִילּוּי רַב וְעָצוּם דְּהַיְינוּ

---

tual version of *Yalkut Shimoni, Tehillim,*
sect. 494. See the Rebbe's footnote in *Sefer Hamaamarim 5700,* p. 40.

   G-d can only be termed "great" once
He has descended to create the worlds,
"for the 'Essence' of G-d cannot be investigated and deemed 'great.'" Therefore, His "greatness" is an act of "humility," essentially lowering Himself to
become King of the worlds.

65. Psalms 145:13.

66. Ibid. 29:10. Lit., "the L-rd will sit as
the King forever." The Hebrew word
le'olam can mean both "world" and "for-

ever." In order for G-d to be "King of the
world," He "sits"—lowering himself in
order to relate to such lowly matters.

67. Ibid. 22:4.

68. Praises are addressed only to something one can understand and relate to. It
is therefore impossible for Israel to praise
Atzmut, for we cannot relate to or understand G-d's Essence.

69. *Kadosh* can mean both "holy" or
"sanctified" and "separated" or "removed."

the level where "I, G-d, have not changed"—"past, present and future exist at once"[70]—for all flesh shall perceive with physical intellect that G-d will be "revealed," as discussed earlier.[71]

...IN OUR WORLD

Moreover, this manifestation will occur specifically in our lowly, physical world. For as our Sages explain, the verse, "It is asked of Jacob and Israel, 'What has G-d wrought,'"[72] is the question the ministering angels will ask of *tzadikim* (the righteous);[73] and instead of the angels asking, "Where is the place of His glory?",[74] they will answer, "His glory fills the world."[75]

THE CROWN

This is the meaning of the verse, "A woman of excellence is the crown of her husband."[76] The divine radiance that is manifest now to the Jewish people is called "her husband."[77] When Moshiach comes, however, the Jewish people will be of an infinitely greater

---

70. *Zohar* III (*Raya Mehemna*) 257b.

71. At the end of Chapter 2, the *maamar* explained that the distinction between exile and the Messianic Era is marked by whether the divine radiance is manifest or not. Based on what we just explained in Chapter 5 the *maamar* makes the distinction even bolder, by saying that not only will *divine radiance* (*giluyim*) be manifest in the Future Time (as it is now, during exile, on the Shabbat and festivals), but *G-d Himself*, i.e. G-d's *Essence* (*Atzmut*), will then be revealed.

72. Numbers 23:23.

73. *Midrash Tanchuma, Balak* 14; *Bamidbar Rabbah* 20:20; Rashi on Numbers ibid.

When G-d's Essence will be manifest in creation in the Messianic Age, the heavenly angels will wonder why is it that G-d is showing Himself to mortal man, as

opposed to the more "supernal" realms. Thus, it is evident that this revelation will be exclusively in the lowest of worlds —ours.

74. Liturgy, Shabbat *Musaf* prayer. See also *Zohar* III (*Raya Mehemna*) 82a and 281a.

75. Isaiah 6:3.

76. Proverbs 12:4. Kabbalistic texts explain this verse to be referring to the state of affairs in the Messianic Era, when the Jewish people will be raised to a tremendous spiritual standing, a level that surpasses even that of the divine radiance that presently emanates life.

77. "HUSBAND"—"WIFE" (MASCULINE —FEMININE / MASHPIA—MEKABEL): In general these denote the aspects of the active, emanating (influencing) category and the passive, receiving qualities and cat-

הַמְשָׁכַת אֱלֹקוּתוֹ יִתְבָּרֵךְ וְעַצְמוּתוֹ וּמַהוּתוֹ מִבְּחִינַת אֲנִי
ה' לֹא שָׁנִיתִי הָיָה הֹוֶה וְיִהְיֶה בְּרֶגַע אֶחָד וְרָאוּ כָל בָּשָׂר
בְּעֵינֵי הַשֵּׂכֶל גַּשְׁמִי כִּי אֱלֹהֵינוּ יִהְיֶה בִּבְחִינַת זֶה כַּנִּזְכָּר
לְעֵיל.

וְהִתְגַּלּוּת זֶה יִהְיֶה בַּתַּחְתּוֹנִים דַּוְקָא לְמַטָּה. וּכְמוֹ
שֶׁאָמְרוּ רַבּוֹתֵינוּ זִכְרוֹנָם לִבְרָכָה עַל פָּסוּק כָּעֵת יֵאָמֵר
בְּיַעֲקֹב וּלְיִשְׂרָאֵל מַה פָּעַל אֵל. שֶׁמַּלְאֲכֵי הַשָּׁרֵת יִשְׁאֲלוּ זֹאת
לַצַּדִּיקִים וּבְמָקוֹם שֶׁהָיוּ מַלְאֲכֵי הַשָּׁרֵת אוֹמְרִים אַיֵּה
מְקוֹם כְּבוֹדוֹ יֹאמְרוּ מְלֹא כָל הָאָרֶץ כְּבוֹדוֹ.

וְזֶהוּ אֵשֶׁת חַיִל עֲטֶרֶת בַּעְלָהּ שֶׁאוֹר ה' הַמִּתְגַּלֶּה בָהּ

---

egories, the mode or form of emanation-reception and so forth (see bi-lingual ed. *Iggeret Hakodesh*, section 15, note 9). In our context, the divine "emanating" energy is called *ba'al* (husband), a masculine term, while the "receptive" souls of Israel are called *isha* (a woman), a feminine term.

These ideas are found in many places throughout Kabbalah: "The whole universe functions according to the principium of masculine and feminine" (*Etz Chaim* 11:6). "There are four principles: masculine and feminine; judgment (*din*) and compassion (*rachamim*); upper and lower; influencer or emanator (*mashpia*) and influenced (*mushpa*; also called *mekabel*—recipient). As a rule, the masculine corresponds to compassion, upper and emanator; and the feminine corresponds to judgment, lower and recipient," idem., *Pri Etz Chaim, Hakdamah* II:end of *D'rush* 2 (ed. Tel Aviv 1966, p. 13a), and *Olat Tamid*, beg. of *Shaar Hatefillah* (ed. Tel Aviv 1963, p. 2a).

Actually, such terminology is not uniquely Kabbalistic. It may be found in Talmudic sources, such as *Bava Batra* 74b: "All that the Holy One, blessed is He, created in His world, He created male and female" (see the commentaries ad loc., and esp., *Chidushei Harashba* at *Agadot Hashas*, op. cit., pp. 91 ff., quoted at length by Rabbi Jacob ibn Chabib in his *Hakotev* on *Ein Yaakov*), as well as in philosophical literature, e.g., *Moreh Nevuchim*, Introduction, and ibid., I; ch. 6 and 17, and III; ch. 8 and 12.

Rabbi Schneur Zalman explains at length why the mystics purposely chose such delicate and seemingly peculiar terminology; see *Likkutei Torah, Shir Hashirim* 9a, and R. DovBer, *Biurei HaZohar, Noach* pp. 6a-ff (Kehot, 1955). The earlier mystics, too, elaborate on the usage of these particular concepts. See *Pardess Rimonim* 32:1; *Shiur Komah*, ch. 18; *Sh'nei Luchot HaBrit*, ad loc. cit. (p. 8d ff.); *Shomer Emunim* I:26f.

spiritual standing [than "her husband," the divine radiance, for then they will see the Essence of G-d Himself].[78]

STABILITY

It is thus written, "The maiden of Israel has fallen, she will no longer rise":[79] The world will be so completely permeated with G-dliness that it will not be necessary for Israel to "rise" [in order to experience spirituality].[80]

7.

TRANSFORMATION

The reason why it will be possible to have such a powerful manifestation in our lowly realm in the Messianic Era is because then, unlike the previous redemptions where the evil was merely subjugated and broken, "*le'achfaya le'sitra achara*," the darkness itself will be transformed to light.[81]

Regarding the past redemptions, scripture uses phrases like, "Who struck Egypt through its firstborn," and "And slew mighty kings,"[82] statements indicating that the evil was subdued and destroyed. Speaking of the future redemption, in contrast, the verse says, "For then I will *transform* the nations to speak a pure language, [so that they all will proclaim the Name of G-d, to worship Him in unison],"[83] "And many nations will go [and say, 'Come, let us go up

---

78. The verse therefore states regarding the Messianic Age, "A woman of excellence is the crown of her husband"—for just as a crown lies above the head, so too will Israel then be (spiritually) "above" the manifestation of G-dliness that is now termed *ba'alah*.

79. Amos 5:2. At first glance, the verse appears to be saying that Israel will never rise from exile and be redeemed, G-d forbid—something that contradicts one of the most fundamental beliefs of Judaism. The *maamar* therefore explains the deeper meaning of this prophecy, to actually be speaking of the Messianic Era.

[For a more literal explanation of this verse, see Rashi ("There will no longer be a king rising from the ten tribes"); *Radak* ("Israel will not rise for a long time"); *Metzudat David* ibid.

Alternatively, the Talmud (*Berachot* 4b) relates that this phrase may be repunctuated and read as a message of encouragement: "She has fallen but will no longer; rise up, maiden of Israel!"]

80. Now, during exile, when one wishes to draw nearer to G-d, one must rise up from the coarse, physical elements that keep one fettered to materiality. When Moshiach comes, however, there will be

עַכְשָׁיו נִקְרָא בַּעְלָה. אֲבָל לֶעָתִיד יִהְיֶה בְּמַדְרֵגָה גְּבוֹהַ
יוֹתֵר.

לָכֵן כְּתִיב נָפְלָה לֹא תוֹסִיף קוּם בְּתוּלַת יִשְׂרָאֵל.
פֵּירוּשׁ שֶׁלֹּא יִהְיֶה שַׁיָּיךְ לָהּ בְּחִינַת קִימָה וַעֲלִיָּיה כִּי יִהְיֶה
אוֹר ה' בְּגִילּוּי רַב לְמַטָּה דַּוְקָא.

ז.

וְהַיְינוּ מִשּׁוּם שֶׁאִתְהַפְּכָא חֲשׁוֹכָא לִנְהוֹרָא וְלֹא
לְאַכְפְּיָיא לְסִטְרָא אָחֳרָא בִּלְבָד לְבַטְּלָם וּלְהַכְנִיעָם

כְּמוֹ בִּשְׁאָר גָּלוּת דִּכְתִיב לְמַכֵּה מִצְרַיִם בִּבְכוֹרֵיהֶם

---

no need to "rise up," for G-d's Essence will be found here, in this world.

81. IT'KAFIA – IT'HAPCHA: Lit., subjugation and transformation. *It'kafia* refers to the state in which the forces of evil and *kelipah* are subdued and controlled by the forces of *kedusha* (spirituality), while *it'hapcha* speaks of the state in which *kelipah* has been transformed to good.

Throughout history, when the forces of spirituality prevailed over *kelipah*, it was in a manner of *it'kafia*: evil remained—it was just subjugated and broken by *kedusha*. [Even when the nations conceded the truth, as did Egypt after the ten plagues (as it says, "And Egypt will know that I am G-d"), and as it was during King Solomon's rule, when the nations sent offerings and gifts to the Holy Temple, it did not represent a transformation of their attitude and sentiment, but was rather a coerced reflex to those particular situations. (*Maamarei Admur Ha'emtza'ee*, pp. 399-400.)

In the Future Time, however, *kelipah* itself will be utterly transformed to *kedusha*.

Therefore, in the time preceding the arrival of Moshiach, G-dliness cannot be manifest in the world, for though the elements of evil and darkness are subdued, their mere existence obscures divinity to a certain extent. The only way to perceive spirituality is to elevate oneself and ascend higher and higher. When Moshiach comes, however, the darkness will turn to light, and thus, G-d Himself will be revealed here, in our world.

82. Psalms 136:18

83. Zephaniah 3:9.

to the Mountain of G-d … that He may teach us of His ways and we may walk in His paths.'"[84] For at that time, the darkness will turn to light.]

AHASUERUS' CHANGE OF HEART

Now we can understand why amongst the Jewish festivals, only Purim will remain a holiday in the Messianic Age, for the miracle of Purim embodied a similar transformation, that of King Ahasuerus' heart: The very same mouth that gave Haman the authority to decree the destruction of the Jewish people, G-d forbid, saying, "The nation is yours, [Haman,] to do with as you please,"[85] eventually granted Esther and Mordechai the power to "issue decrees concerning the Jews as you please."[86] This is the idea of "darkness being transformed into light," as it will be in the time of Moshiach, when "the glory of the L-rd shall be revealed" specifically in the darkest, lowliest realm.[87]

8.

SHEDDING LIGHT ON HALACHAH

This is also why our sages say that *halachah,* Jewish law, will never be abolished, for it also embodies the "transformation of darkness to light."

To explain: On the verse, "Flee, my beloved, and be like a gazelle,"[88] the Sages comment: "Just as a gazelle turns its head backwards [even as it flees, so does Israel say to G-d: 'Master of the Universe, if we have caused that You should remove Your presence from amongst us, may it be Your Will that You should be as a gazelle, who flees and yet turns it head back to where it left]."[89]

---

84. Isaiah 2:3.

85. Esther 3:11.

86. Ibid. 8:8.

87. Earlier, the *maamar* explained two points regarding the Messianic Age: one,

that that the novelty of Moshiach's arrival is that then, G-d Himself will be manifest in this world (Chapter 6), and two, that this revelation is dependant on *it'hapcha,* the transformation of darkness to light (Chapter 7). Now, when wishing to demonstrate the correlation between Purim and the Messianic Era (to

וגו'. וַיַּהֲרֹג מְלָכִים אַדִּירִים וגו'. רַק כִּי גַם אָז אֶהְפֹּךְ אֶל
עַמִּים שָׂפָה בְרוּרָה וגו' וְהָלְכוּ עַמִּים רַבִּים וגו'.

וְהִנֵּה מֵעֵין זֶה הָיָה הַנֵּס שֶׁל פּוּרִים שֶׁנִּתְהַפֵּךְ לֵב
אֲחַשְׁוֵרוֹשׁ לְטוֹב. אוֹתוֹ הַפֶּה עַצְמוֹ שֶׁאָמַר וְהָעָם
לַעֲשׂוֹת בּוֹ כַּטּוֹב בְּעֵינֶיךָ הוּא עַצְמוֹ אָמַר וְאַתֶּם כִּתְבוּ
עַל הַיְּהוּדִים כַּטּוֹב בְּעֵינֵיכֶם. שֶׁהוּא עִנְיָן אִתְהַפְּכָא
חֲשׁוֹכָא לִנְהוֹרָא וְנִגְלָה כְּבוֹד ה' לְמַטָּה בִּמְקוֹם הַחֹשֶׁךְ
דַּוְקָא:

.ח

וְלָכֵן אָמְרוּ רַבּוֹתֵינוּ זִכְרוֹנָם לִבְרָכָה שֶׁגַּם הֲלָכוֹת
אֵינָן בְּטֵלוֹת.

וּבֵיאוּר הָעִנְיָן כִּי הִנֵּה אָמְרוּ רַבּוֹתֵינוּ זִכְרוֹנָם
לִבְרָכָה עַל פָּסוּק בְּרַח דּוֹדִי וּדְמֵה לְךָ לִצְבִי וגו' מַה צְּבִי
מַחֲזִיר רֹאשׁוֹ לַאֲחוֹרָיו.

---

explain why Purim will never be abolished), the *maamar* notes only one sim-
ilarity—that Purim also contains the
idea of *it'hapcha*. Later, in Chapter 10,
the fact that the miracle of Purim also
represents the manifestation of G-d's Essence (as opposed to mere revelation)
will also be demonstrated, thus com-
pleting the comparison.

88. Song of Songs 8:14.

89. *Zohar* II:14a. The simple interpretation of this *Zohar* is that it is referring to the relationship between the
divine presence and the Jewish People
during exile—even though we are in exile, we ask that G-d still shine His presence amongst us. The *maamar*, however, interprets it as also referring to the
implementation of the divine will and
wisdom into *halachah*, as will soon be
demonstrated.

THE HEAD

To understand this, we can bring an analogy: Man's skull contains his brain, his intellect and his understanding. When he turns his head backward, then his brain and mind that are contained within follow suit.

'PHYSICAL' LAW

The same is true in a spiritual sense: G-d "turned His head back" so to speak, and placed His will and wisdom in the "back," in those things that are considered *chitzoniyut* (external)—i.e., in physical, material matters.[90] *Seder Kodshim,*[91] for example, discusses animal [sacrifices], and *Seder Nezikin* deals with monetary issues. Thus, G-d's deepest will and wisdom is garbed within the "physical" laws of the Torah. Moreover, His emotive attributes, or *middot,* are also drawn to *halachah,* as it says, "He has drawn back His right hand."[92]

---

90. *Halachah* is the will and wisdom of G-d: "For such is the will and wisdom of the Holy One, blessed be He, that in the event of a person pleading this way and the other [litigant] pleading that way, the verdict shall be such and such" (*Tanya,* Chapter 5). Yet, all of the *halachot* that are found within the *Mishnah* and Talmud deal with physical, mundane matters.

In Chasidic terminology, physicality is considered to be *achorayim* (the "back") and *chitzoniyut* ("external" or "indirect"), since it is naturally "distant" from G-d's will, while spirituality is termed *panim* (the "face") and *p'nimiyut* ("internal" or "direct"), being naturally "nearer" to that which G-d desires.

To explain these terms, Rabbi Schneur Zalman writes the following (*Tanya,* Chapter 22): "The meaning of the term *achorayim* ("back") is like a person giving something unwillingly to an enemy, whereby he throws it over his shoulder, having turned his face from him because

of his hatred.

"Similarly above, the term *panim* (face) denotes the inner quality (*p'nimiyut*) of the supernal will and G-d's true desire, in which G-d delights in giving life from the realm of holiness to all who are near Him.

"But the negative and unholy forces are 'an abomination unto G-d, which He hates,' and He does not give it life from His inner will and true desire as if He delighted in it, G-d forbid, but rather as one who reluctantly throws something over his shoulder to his enemy ... This is why it is called *achorayim* (the "back") of the divine will."

Thus, *halacha,* since it concerns mundane matters, is considered to be *achorayim* and *chitzoniyut.*

91. The *Mishnah* is divided into six "orders" or "categories." They are: *Zera'im* (Plants), *Moed* (Festivals), *Nashim* (Women), *Nezikin* (Damages), *Kodshim* (Sanctities), *Taharot* (Purities). Each of these orders contains a number of tractates that

דְּהַיְינוּ עַל דֶּרֶךְ מָשָׁל כְּמוֹ שֶׁבָּאָדָם בְּעֶצֶם רֹאשׁוֹ
הִנֵּה מוּנָח בְּתוֹכוֹ מוֹחַ וְשִׂכְלוֹ וּבִינָתוֹ וּכְשֶׁמַּחֲזִיר עֶצֶם
רֹאשׁוֹ לַאֲחוֹרָיו הִנֵּה גַּם הַמּוֹחַ אֲשֶׁר בְּתוֹכוֹ וְרוּחַ
שִׂכְלוֹ וּבִינָתוֹ נִמְשָׁכִין אַחֲרָיו

כָּךְ כִּבְיָכוֹל הַמָּשִׁיךְ הַקָּדוֹשׁ בָּרוּךְ הוּא וְהִלְבִּישׁ
רְצוֹנוֹ וְחָכְמָתוֹ בְּמָקוֹם אֲחוֹרָיו שֶׁהֵם בְּחִינַת חִיצוֹנִיּוּת
דְּהַיְינוּ בְּעִנְיָנִים גַּשְׁמִיִּים כְּמוֹ בִּבְהֵמוֹת בְּסֵדֶר קָדָשִׁים.
וּבְמָעוֹת בְּסֵדֶר נְזִיקִין. דִּפְנִימִית רְצוֹנוֹ וְחָכְמָתוֹ
יִתְבָּרֵךְ מְלוּבָּשִׁים בָּהֶם וְגַם מִדּוֹתָיו יִתְבָּרֵךְ הֵם נִמְשָׁכִים
אַחֲרֵיהֶם מֵאֲלֵיהֶם וּמִמֵּילָא כְּמוֹ שֶׁכָּתוּב הֵשִׁיב אָחוֹר
יְמִינוֹ וגו'.

---

discuss various laws generally pertaining to a specific topic of the given category.

92. Lamentations 2:3.
"His right hand" refers to the divine attribute of *chesed* (loving-kindness) — *Tikunei Zohar*, introduction, 17a. Thus, the verse is saying that G-d has invested His emotive attributes (such as *chesed*) in the "back," in the mundane, physical technicalities of *halachah*.

Middot (emotions) naturally follow *sechel* (intellect). For example, when a person understands that a certain thing will cause him pleasure, there will automatically be born within him a feeling of desire for that thing; such is the nature of man. Similarly, G-d's supernal *middot* naturally follow His will and wisdom. Therefore, when He garbs His will and wisdom in physical *halachah*, His *middot* naturally follow suit.

The function of *middot* within *halachah* is to aid in determining the verdict of a given scenario when there is merit to both arguments. Determining whether something is permissible or forbidden, pure or impure, liable or justified, is affected by one's *middot*: *chesed* (kindness) naturally leans toward a lenient judgment, while *gevurah* (severity) leans toward a more stringent judgment.

There are instances where the same objective, logical argument could produce two opposite conclusions, based on one's subjective feelings. To cite an example: In Genesis 6:5, G-d decides to destroy the earth, for "the product of the thoughts of [man's] heart was but always evil." After the flood, G-d promises to never again destroy the world, for "the imagery of man's heart is evil from his youth" (ibid. 8:21)—the very same reason that He originally gave for its destruction! Thus, the fact that man is evil by nature can be used both as a reason to punish and as an excuse to forgive. This, then, is the function of *middot* in *halachah*: to sway an objective, neutral thought toward a certain direction.

DIVINE DECIPHER

Thus, "They [good and evil] are separated through *chochmah*, wisdom."[93] The term "separating" applies to a mixture of two like items that might ordinarily be indistinguishable. [In our context, this means that the "wisdom" of Torah distinguishes between that which is *halachah*, and that which is not, something not always easily discernable.]

THE FINE LINE

An agent who "exchanges a cow for a donkey" in a business deal,[94] or a butcher that is cutting up an animal and gutting its insides for his livelihood, is not involved with the divine will and wisdom. But one who is involved with these very acts for the purpose of discerning the *halachic* ramifications therein—to examine the parts of the animal to determine if it is kosher or not, to determine who is meritorious and who is liable in the dispute over a newly born calf, and, in the laws of ritual purity, to determine what is pure and what is impure—is thereby touching upon the divine will and wisdom of G-d.

Similarly, the sages of the *Mishnah* and Talmud, and the earlier and latter *Poskim*,[95] clarified and revealed the divine will and wisdom, and thus "separated" the evil from the good. Through their Torah study they distinguished that which is not permissible from that which is permissible, and [in matters of civil law,] the one who is found liable from the one who is found meritorious.

A TEST OF CHARACTER

Similarly in practical mitzvot that are connected with one's good character:[96] There is a general principal that one who is occupied with a *mitzvah* is free from the obligation of performing other *mitzvot*.[97] Therefore, one who found a lost article and is currently fulfilling the *mitzvah* of caring for that article by "spreading it out

---

93. *Zohar* II (*heichalot*) 254b; *Etz Chaim, Shaar* 18, Chapter 5; *Shaar* 39, *D'rush* 1.

94. *Mishnah, Bava Metzia* 8:4.

The *Mishnah's* case is this: Reuven owns a cow and Shimon owns a donkey, both of equal value. They decide to trade

their possessions—Reuven acquiring the donkey, and Shimon taking the cow. After the swap is made, they realize that the cow gave birth, but they are unsure as to whether the calf was born before the deal was finalized, and thus, belongs to Reuven, or if it was born after the deal

וּבְחָכְמָה אִתְבְּרִירוּ פֵּירוּשׁ כִּי אֵין לְשׁוֹן בֵּירוּר נוֹפֵל
אֶלָּא בְּדָבָר שֶׁמִּתְעָרֵב כְּגוֹן מִין בְּמִינוֹ וְאֵינוֹ נִיכָּר.

כַּךְ עַל דֶּרֶךְ מָשָׁל סַרְסוּר הַמַּחֲלִיף פָּרָה בַּחֲמוֹר לְגַבֵּי
הַשּׁוֹנֶה מִשְׁנָה וַהֲלָכָה בְּנִתּוּחַ
אֶבְרֵי הַבְּהֵמָה לִנְתָחִים וּבִבְנֵי מֵעַיִם וְכוּ' הוּא קַצָּב. אַךְ
הַמִּתְעַסֵּק לֵידַע כָּל פְּרָטֵי הֲלָכוֹת הַתְּלוּיִין בְּאֶבְרֵי הַבְּהֵמָה
לְהַבְדִּיל בֵּין טְרֵפָה לַכְּשֵׁרָה וְכֵן בְּמַחֲלִיף פָּרָה לֵידַע
וּלְהַבְדִּיל וּלְבָרֵר בֵּין חַיָּיב לְזַכַּאי וְכֵן בְּסֵדֶר טְהָרוֹת בֵּין
טָמֵא לַטָהוֹר כו'.

וְכֵן בְּכָל שִׁתָּא סִדְרֵי מִשְׁנָה וּגְמָרָא וְכָל הַפּוֹסְקִים
רִאשׁוֹנִים וְאַחֲרוֹנִים מִתְגַּלֶּה וּמִתְבָּרֵר רָצוֹן הָעֶלְיוֹן
וְחָכְמָתוֹ יִתְבָּרֵךְ וְעַל יְדֵי זֶה מִתְבָּרֵר וְנִפְרָד הָרָע מֵהַטוֹב
דְּהַיְינוּ הַפָּסוּל מֵהַכָּשֵׁר וְחַיָּיב מִזַכַּאי

וְכֵן בְּמִצְוֹת מַעֲשִׂיּוֹת הַתְּלוּיִין בְּמִדּוֹת כְּגוֹן שׁוֹמֵר
אֲבֵידָה שֶׁפָּטוּר לִיתֵּן פְּרוּטָה לְעָנִי. שֶׁעוֹסֵק בְּמִצְוָה פָּטוּר
מִמִּצְוָה. וְהַיְינוּ אִם עוֹסֵק בָּה לְצָרְכָּה לְשָׁטְחָה וּלְנַעֲרָה

---

was made, thus, belonging to Shimon. Each party claims the calf to be theirs. The *halachah*? They sell the calf and split its value equally. [*Rambam* (*Hilchot Mechirah* 20:10, 11) explains that the *halachah* would only be so in a case where both claim to be *unsure* of the calf's status. If, however, both claim to be the rightful owner, the calf would then belong to the original owner of the cow, Reuven.]

95. *Poskim* (sing. *Posek*) is the general ti-

tle given to the Torah personalities who developed Jewish law through the ages. The "earlier" *Poskim*, or *Rishonim*, lived between c. 1000-1500 C.E., while the "latter" *Poskim*, or *Achronim*, lived between c. 1500-1800 C.E.

96. I.e., the same action can either be considered to be a *mitzvah* or not, depending upon under what circumstances it was done.

97. *Sukkah* 25a.

and shaking it,"[98] does not have to give charity at that time,[99] for by taking care of another's property, regardless of the owner's financial status, he is performing a *mitzvah*. One, however, who is caring for his own items, is not fulfilling a *mitzvah*—though he may be a pauper. Thus, he would be obligated to perform other *mitzvot*.

Likewise, one who gives charity is performing a *mitzvah*, while one who spends money on personal matters is not. [This is the fine line that *halachah* delineates.]

THE BOTTOM LINE

So when one performs a *mitzvah* with a material object, it is in effect transforming darkness to light, causing the G-dly radiance of the divine will to shine specifically in the darkness of materiality.[100]

9.

A 'SPACE' FOR G-D

This is the meaning of the verse, "Behold, He (*zeh*) stands behind our wall [watching through the windows, peering through the crevices]"[101]:

VISUAL IMPAIRMENT

Although the divine wisdom and will is manifest in Torah matters, in the manner of *zeh*, it nonetheless "stands behind our wall", i.e., we cannot perceive the G-dly radiance of Torah and *mitzvot*. This lack of perception stems from our sins, which act as a wall to impede this radiance from shining.[102]

---

98. *Mishnah, Bava Metzia* 2:8. The *Mishnah* is referring to a lost garment; by "spreading it out and shaking it," one helps to air out and preserve the garment.

See also *Shulchan Aruch* of Rabbi Schneur Zalman (*Hilchot Metziah u'Pikadon*, para. 24): "From where do we know that one must take precaution with a lost object to prevent it from getting ruined and destroyed? For it says, "And you shall return it to him"—it is only proper that you return it to him in perfect

condition. And while one is minding a lost object, one is "occupied with a *mitzvah*" and as such does not have to give bread to a pauper or perform other *mitzvot*..."

99. *Bava Kama* 56b; Rashi ibid.

100. When one is occupied with *halachah*, he is essentially taking practical, everyday, physical matters that appear to be nothing more than just that, and transforming them into vehicles through

וְאֵין חִילוּק בֵּין הִיא אֲבֵדַת עָשִׁיר אוֹ עָנִי. מַה שֶׁאֵין כֵּן
אִם שׁוֹמֵר כְּסוּת שֶׁלּוֹ אֲפִילוּ אֵינוֹ עָשִׁיר כְּמוֹ בַּעַל
אֲבֵדָה הֲרֵי אֵין בּוֹ מִצְוָה.

וְכֵן הָעִנְיָן בִּצְדָקָה וּגְמִילוּת חֲסָדִים מַה שֶׁעוֹשֶׂה חֶסֶד
עִם הַבְּרִיּוֹת הֲרֵי זֶה מִצְוָה. וְאִם עוֹשֶׂה לְצָרְכּוֹ אֵין בּוֹ
מִצְוָה.

וְאִם כֵּן כְּשֶׁעוֹשֶׂה מִצְוָה בְּדָבָר גַּשְׁמִי הֲרֵי הוּא עִנְיָן
הַהִתְהַפְּכוּת חֲשׁוֹכָא לִנְהוֹרָא שֶׁאוֹר ה' הוּא גִּילּוּי רְצוֹנוֹ
יִתְבָּרֵךְ וְאוֹר בִּמְקוֹם הַחֹשֶׁךְ הַגַּשְׁמִי דַּוְקָא:

ט.

וְזֶהוּ הִנֵּה זֶה עוֹמֵד אַחַר כָּתְלֵנוּ.

פֵּירוּשׁ בְּחִינַת חָכְמָתוֹ וּרְצוֹנוֹ יִתְבָּרֵךְ הוּא בְּחִינַת
הִתְגַּלּוּת בִּבְחִינַת זֶה בְּעִנְיְנֵי הַתּוֹרָה אֶלָּא שֶׁעוֹמֵד אַחַר
כָּתְלֵנוּ שֶׁאֵין אוֹר ה' שׁוֹרֶה וּמִתְגַּלֶּה בּוֹ מִפְּנֵי
שֶׁעֲוֹנוֹתֵיכֶם מַבְדִּילִין וְעוֹמֵד לְנֶגְדּוֹ בַּכּוֹתֶל.

---

which the divine will and wisdom are clarified.

Hence *halachah* will never be abolished, for it too embodies the Messianic theme of transforming darkness into light.

101. Song of Songs 2:9.

The *maamar* is addressing the obvious question: If there is this "transformation of darkness to light" in *halachah*, then one who deals with *halachah* should be able to literally perceive G-dliness (like the revela-

tion of "the glory of G-d" in the Messianic Era). Why is it then, that when we occupy ourselves with *halachah* we still do not perceive divinity?

The answer is that it is our sins and ego that stand in the way of this revelation, and thus, it is up to us to remove the impediments.

102. It is therefore called "*our* wall," for it is we who construct it, through our sins—*Maamarei Admur Ha'emtza'ee*, p. 508.

THE SOLUTION—HUMILITY

The solution to this problem is found in the words "watching through the windows, peering through the crevices." Windows and crevices are both created by carving holes into a wall—the only difference is one of size. Similarly, when one's heart is as spiritually sensitive as a cold, hard "stone,"[103] one must then "carve out" space within it, as our sages say, "open for Me the point of a needle [and I will open for you the most spacious of chambers]."[104] One needs to break the spirit of haughtiness that covers the heart, to make "a contrite spirit, a broken heart,"[105] for the "wall" that stands between man and G-d is in reality one's ego, the self-centeredness that gives more significance to personal matters than spiritual affairs.[106]

10.

Now we can return to the story of Esther.

ESTHER APPROACHES…

When King Ahasuerus initially saw her she was "standing in the courtyard."[107] Metaphorically speaking, this refers to the soul's initial spiritual posture, as it "rises from the wilderness" of negativity; for even when the soul stands in the "inner courtyard"[108] of the King, it is still a "wilderness" compared to where He permanently resides.[109] [The soul thus stands in the "courtyard," in this spiritual wasteland, yearning to rise up and be together with the King.][110] Then, there is a manifestation of divine radiance showered upon the soul, which

---

103. Cf. Ezekiel 11:19 and 36:26.

104. See *Shir Hashirim Rabbah* 5:2.

105. Psalms 51:19.

106. One who is narcissistic by definition cares more about personal matters than anything else—even G-d.

107. Esther 5:2.

108. Ibid. 5:1.

109. There is a parallel between the

"courtyard" mentioned in the story of Esther and the spiritual *midbar* ("wilderness") that every soul finds itself in (as a result of its descent into a physical world): Just as a *midbar* is devoid of civilization, alluding to a state that is devoid of spirituality, similarly, a courtyard—even the "inner courtyard" that Esther was standing in—is a place where the king does not permanently dwell, signifying likewise a lack of divine presence.

We explained before (Chapters 3 and 4) that on Shabbat and festivals there is a

וְהָעֵצָה הַיְעוּצָה לָזֶה מַשְׁגִּיחַ מִן הַחַלּוֹנוֹת מֵצִיץ מִן
הַחֲרַכִּים. כִּי חַלּוֹן הוּא חָלָל שֶׁנַּעֲשֶׂה בַּכּוֹתֶל. וְכֵן עִנְיַן
הַחֲרַכִּים אֶלָּא שֶׁחֲרַכִּים הֵם סְדָקִים קְטַנִּים וְחַלּוֹן הוּא
חָלָל גָּדוֹל יוֹתֵר. כַּךְ עַל דֶּרֶךְ מָשָׁל הִנֵּה אָמְרוּ רַבּוֹתֵינוּ
זִכְרוֹנָם לִבְרָכָה פִּתְחִי לִי כְּחוּדָּהּ שֶׁל מַחַט כו'. דְּהַיְינוּ
שֶׁיִּשָּׁבוֹר לִבּוֹ לֵב הָאֶבֶן לִהְיוֹת לוֹ רוּחַ נִשְׁבָּרָה לֵב
נִשְׁבָּר כִּי כָּל הַמָּסְכִים וְהַכּוֹתֶל וְהַמְּחִיצָה הַמַּפְסֶקֶת בֵּינוֹ
לְאָבִיו שֶׁבַּשָּׁמַיִם הוּא בְּחִינַת גַּסֵּי הָרוּחַ אֲשֶׁר עַל כֵּן
מַחֲשַׁב עַצְמוֹ לְיֵשׁ. וְחֶפְצֵי עַצְמוֹ יְקָרִים בְּעֵינָיו מֵחֶפְצֵי
שָׁמַיִם:

י.

וְעִם כָּל הַנִּזְכָּר לְעֵיל יוּבַן וִיבוֹאַר הֵיטֵב עִנְיַן אֶסְתֵּר

שֶׁמִּתְּחִלָּה בִּרְאוֹתוֹ אֶת הַמַּלְכָּה עוֹמֶדֶת בֶּחָצֵר הָיָה
בְּחִינַת זֹאת עוֹלָה מִן הַמִּדְבָּר הַנִּזְכָּר לְעֵיל. כִּי גַם בְּחִינַת
חָצֵר הַפְּנִימִית לְמִדְבָּר יֵחָשֵׁב נֶגֶד בֵּית הַמֶּלֶךְ מַמָּשׁ לְפִי
שֶׁאֵין הַמֶּלֶךְ דָּר בִּקְבִיעוּת בֶּחָצֵר כְּמוֹ בַּבַּיִת אֲזַי מִתְגַּלֶּה

---

manifestation of divine radiance that causes the Jewish people to rise from the grip of materiality and ascend to spiritual heights. Similarly, in the story of Esther, after she (the soul) stood in the courtyard (the "grip of materiality") and yearned to see the king (G-d), He "extended to Esther the golden scepter that was in his hand," manifesting G-dly radiance upon the soul, allowing it to rise higher and higher in its spiritual quest and to develop a divine, G-dly passion.

Nonetheless, like on Shabbat and festivals, this is how the soul experiences *G-dliness* (divine manifestation, *giluyim*) —but not *G-d Himself* (*Atzmut*). That is why the verse says that Esther merely "touched the *tip* of the scepter," as the *maamar* will soon note.

110. While Haman—the element of evil—still exists, the only way to "approach the King" is by detaching and rising from those forces. Thus, the soul stands in the "courtyard" and yearns to be with the King, to be united with G-d.

enables it to ascend and approach the King with immense passion, as it says, "And Esther approached."[111]

But even after the soul has ascended to spiritual heights and "approached" divinity, it is still considered to be merely touching the "tip of the scepter."[112]

...AND ARRIVES

Afterwards, however, when she was in the actual palace where the king resided, "Esther again spoke before the king and fell before his feet, and she cried and begged him to nullify the evil decree of Haman the Agagite, and his plot that he had plotted against the Jews."[113] In reference to the soul, its crying is to arouse G-d's abundant mercy, to have compassion on the spark of divinity that is trapped and garbed within the arrogance of one's corporeal self[114]—"the evil decree of Haman … that he had plotted against the Jews." For from Haman come these [narcissistic] thoughts.[115]

Then, the soul has transformed darkness into light.[116]

That is why "the king extended the golden scepter to Esther" in its entirety,[117] for when darkness is transformed to light, G-d's Essence can be manifest in this world.[118]

---

111. Ibid 5:2.

112. See Chapter 5.

113. Esther 8:3.

114. See *Tanya*, Chapter 45: "There is yet another direct road open to man [to attain a great love of G-d]... it is to first arouse in his mind great compassion before G-d for the divine spark that animates his soul that has descended from its source, the Life of life... Yet [this spark] has been clothed in a 'serpent's skin' which is removed from the light of the King's countenance, at the greatest possible distance, since this world is the nadir of the coarse *kelipot*... And especially

when he will recall all his actions and utterances and thoughts since the day he came into being, unworthy as they were, causing the King to be 'fettered by the tresses' (Song of Songs 7:6)..."

115. Haman descended from Amalek, a nation that epitomized haughtiness. When the Jewish people left Egypt amidst tremendous miracles, all of the nations of the world feared them, sensing the hand of G-d guiding their destiny—all but Amalek, whose arrogance defied logic and caused them to provoke Israel into battle, a battle they ultimately lost.

In the microcosm of man, there too exists this Amalek/Haman element of arrogance, which impedes spiritual growth.

הָאָרַת וְהַמְשָׁכַת אוֹר ה׳. וְאָז וַתִּקְרַב אֶסְתֵּר שֶׁמִּתְעַלָּה וּמִתְקָרֶבֶת אֶל הַמֶּלֶךְ בִּתְשׁוּקָה לְדוֹדָהּ.

אֲבָל כָּל הָעֲלִיּוֹת וְהִתְקָרְבוּת אֵינוֹ אֶלָּא וַתִּגַּע בְּרֹאשׁ הַשַּׁרְבִיט.

אֲבָל אַחֲרֵי כֵן כְּתִיב וַתּוֹסֶף אֶסְתֵּר וְגו׳ דְּהַיְינוּ בִּהְיוֹתָהּ אִתּוֹ בַּבַּיִת וַתֵּבְךְ וַתִּתְחַנֶּן לוֹ לְהַעֲבִיר אֶת רָעַת הָמָן הָאֲגָגִי אֲשֶׁר חָשַׁב עַל הַיְּהוּדִים. שֶׁהַבְּכִיָּה הִיא לְעוֹרֵר רַחֲמִים רַבִּים עַל נִצוֹץ אֱלֹהוּת אֲשֶׁר נִתְלַבֵּשׁ בִּלְבוּשִׁים גַּסֵּי הָרוּחַ מִבְּחִינַת הָמָן אֲשֶׁר הוּא חָשַׁב עַל הַיְּהוּדִים. כִּי מִמֶּנּוּ בָּאִים לַיְּהוּדִים מַחֲשָׁבוֹת כָּאֵלּוּ.

וְאָז יִתְהַפְּכוּ חֲשׁוֹכָא לִנְהוֹרָא.

וְלָכֵן וַיּוֹשֶׁט הַמֶּלֶךְ לְאֶסְתֵּר אֶת כָּל הַשַּׁרְבִיט הַזָּהָב שֶׁיָּאִיר אוֹר ה׳ בְּגִילּוּי לְמַטָּה דַוְקָא.

In fact, Chasidut explains that arrogance is the source of all of man's negative traits; hence the meaning of "Amalek is the first of the nations." Thus, the soul cries out to G-d with a bitter heart, to shatter this coarse, thick barrier. (See Chapter 9.)

[Although at this point in the *Megillah* Haman has already been hanged, nonetheless, his evil schemes remain "recorded in the book," and can therefore still have a residual affect on us.] (*Maamarei Admur Ha'emtza'ee*, p. 410.)

116. Man's narcissism (darkness) is replaced by spiritual sensitivity (light).

117. Including the "*top of the scepter*," re-

ferring to G-d's Essence, as explained in Chapter 5.

118. See Chapter 7. This, then, answers the question posed at the beginning of the *maamar*:

Initially, when Esther stood in the courtyard of the king and yearned to approach him—like a soul beginning its spiritual ascent on the Shabbat and festivals—she was only able to touch "the tip of the scepter," to experience the divine *radiance*. Later, when she was in the actual palace, she was able to experience—through her cries to eradicate the evil of Haman (arrogance)—*Atzmut*, G-d's Essence, the *entire* scepter.

ULTIMATE PERFECTION

Subsequently, "Esther rose and stood before the king": The soul is no longer in the process of "ascending from the wilderness," for it has reached the ultimate of spirituality.[119] It is now able to stand prominently "before the king," as it is written, "a woman of excellence is the crown of her husband."[120]

(To[121] better understand the concept of "The king extended…," see what is written [in Likuttei Torah] in Parshat Re'eh on the verse, "When you hearken to the voice…" [23b], and [what is written] in Mikdash Melech, part 1, Parshat Vayechi (228b). Also, the aforementioned maamar entitled "When you hearken…" explains the ideas of "the inner chamber" (chatzer hap'nimit) and "residence" (bayit). To further analyze the concept of bayit, see [Torah Or] Parshat Bereishit, [maamar] entitled, "The heaven is My throne… What house (bayit) [could you build for me]…" [1c]. See also [Torah Or] Parshat Vayeishev in the Haftarah of Chanukah, on the verse, "And you will guard my courtyards," for an alternative explanation.)

---

119. The soul will no longer need to rise, for G-dliness will be manifest in this world—see Chapter 6.

120. I.e., the soul will be on an even greater spiritual plane than that of "her husband," the divine manifestation that is

וְאָז וַתָּקָם אֶסְתֵּר פֵּירוּשׁ שֶׁקָּמָה עַל עָמְדָּהּ וְעַל מַצָּבָהּ
שֶׁלֹּא תִצְטָרֵךְ עוֹד לִבְחִינַת עוֹלָה מִן הַמִּדְבָּר. וְזֶהוּ
וַתַּעֲמוֹד לִפְנֵי הַמֶּלֶךְ שֶׁתְּהֵא בְּמַדְרֵגָה גְדוֹלָה לְפָנָיו
כְּמוֹ שֶׁכָּתוּב אֵשֶׁת חַיִל עֲטֶרֶת בַּעְלָהּ.

(וְעַיֵּן מֵעִנְיָן וַיּוֹשֶׁט הַמֶּלֶךְ כו' בְּמַה שֶׁכָּתוּב פָּרָשַׁת רְאֵה עַל פָּסוּק
כִּי תִשְׁמַע בְּקוֹל כו'. וּבְמִקְדָּשׁ מֶלֶךְ חֵלֶק א' פָּרָשַׁת וַיְחִי (רכ״ח עַמּוּד ב).
גַּם שָׁם בְּדִבּוּר הַמַּתְחִיל כִּי תִשְׁמַע הַנִּזְכָּר לְעֵיל נִתְבָּאֵר עִנְיַן חָצֵר
הַפְּנִימִית וְעִנְיַן בַּיִת. וְעַיֵּן עוֹד מֵעִנְיַן בַּיִת לְעֵיל פָּרָשַׁת בְּרֵאשִׁית בְּדִבּוּר
הַמַּתְחִיל הַשָּׁמַיִם כִּסְאִי כו' אֵי זֶה בַיִת כו' וְעַיֵּן עוֹד לְעֵיל פָּרָשַׁת וַיֵּשֶׁב
בְּהַפְטָרָה דַחֲנוּכָּה עַל פָּסוּק תִּשְׁמוֹר אֶת חֲצֵרָי בְּעִנְיָן אַחֵר):

now transmitted to the soul—ibid.

121. This is a translation of a gloss added
by the *Tzemach Tzedek*, which appears at
the end of the discourse.

BRIEF BIOGRAPHY

BRIEF BIOGRAPHY OF
RABBI SCHNEUR ZALMAN OF LIADI
THE ALTER REBBE
5505-5573 (1745-1812)

BIRTH AND CHILDHOOD

Schneur Zalman (Boruchovitch),[1] who would later come to be known as the *Alter Rebbe* and the *Rav*, was born on the 18th day of *Elul*,[2] in the year 5505 (1745). He was born in Liozna, a small Polish town in the province of Mohilev, lying some 50 miles from the country town of Orsha, on the highway between Smolensk and Vitebsk. His parents, Baruch and Rivkah, had three other sons, all of whom became outstanding Talmudic scholars and held rabbinic posts.[3] Schneur Zalman spent his earliest childhood in the lap of nature, on a fair-sized estate in the vicinity of Liozna operated by his father.

Schneur Zalman's father was apparently a man of some means. He was an imaginative philanthropist, helping a number of Jewish refugee families from Bohemia to settle on the land in the vicinity of Liozna. Baruch himself was born in a family that had originally lived in Bohemia, tracing its ancestry to the famous Rabbi and Kabbalist, Yehuda Lowe of Prague (1512-1609).[4]

---

1. Boruchovitch ("son of Boruch") was Rabbi Schneur Zalman's surname in official Russian documents. His son and successor, Rabbi DovBer, adopted the family name Schneuri. Succeeding generations in line of succession adopted the name Schneersohn, or Schneerson.

2. The 18th of *Elul* is also the birthday of the Baal Shem Tov.

3. Best known of Rabbi Schneur Zal-

man's brothers was Rabbi Yehuda Leib of Yanowitz, author of a *halachic* work, *Sheirit Yehuda* (Kehot, New York, 1957 [2nd ed.]). He recorded many of Rabbi Schneur Zalman's discourses and edited the latter's *Shulchan Aruch* as stated in the preface of that work.

4. The genealogy runs as follows: (1) Yehuda Lowe (Maharal); (2) his son Betzalel; (3) latter's son Shmuel; (4) latter's son Yehuda Leib: (5) his son Moshe: (6)

Rabbi Moshe, the great grandfather of Rabbi Schneur Zalman and a distinguished Talmudist, had lived in the village of Posen. When the so called "Enlightenment" movement began to spread from France eastward with its goal to secularize Judaism, Rabbi Moshe realized its inherent threat and decided to move eastward, beyond the sphere of its evil influence. He packed his belongings and with his entire family wandered through Galicia and Poland in search of a new and proper home. His son, R. Schneur Zalman, finally settled in Vitebsk, then a flourishing center of Torah. There Rabbi Baruch, the father of the *Rav*, was born and reared in the spirit of Torah and its teachings, eventually becoming a great scholar. He later moved to Liozna, a town near Lubavitch,[5] the city that was to become famous as the seat of the dynasty of the *Rav's* descendants.

Baruch was a member of the society of the followers of the Baal Shem Tov, who, at that time, carried on their "missionary" activities among their fellow Jews in secret. So secretive was the work of these *nistarim* (secret mystics) in the early period of the Baal Shem Tov's leadership, that their identity was concealed even from each other. Only the Baal Shem Tov and, later, Baruch's wife Rivkah, knew of Baruch's membership in the *nistarim* society.

Baruch and Rivkah were married on Friday, the 17th of *Elul*, 5503 (1743). When a year had passed by and the young couple was not blessed with a child, Baruch and his wife went to see the Baal Shem Tov to ask him for his blessing.

It was the Baal Shem Tov's custom to celebrate his birthday every year. At the repast on that auspicious day, the 18th of *Elul*, the Baal Shem Tov blessed the couple and promised them that exactly a year later they would become the parents of a boy. Not even the Baal

---

his son Schneur Zalman: (7) his son Boruch, father of Rabbi Schneur Zalman, founder of Chabad.

5. Lubavitch ("Town of Love") in the county of Mohilev, White Russia, has an early history of mystics, the forerunners of the Chasidim. (See *Lubavitcher Rabbi's Memoirs*, Kehot.) It became the residence of the heads of the Chabad-Lubavitch movement in 1814, when Rabbi DovBer, son and successor of Rabbi Schneur Zalman, settled there. For over a century (until 1915) and four generations of Chabad leaders, it remained the center of the movement. Hence the leaders of Chabad became known as the "Lubavitcher Rebbes," and their Chasidim as "Lubavitcher Chasidim."

Shem Tov knew at that time that the soul which was destined to descend into Baruch's son was a new and unblemished soul which had never yet been on earth. Such souls are rare, since most souls descending to earth are reincarnations, sent down to make amends for wrongs or omissions in a life which had once, or even more than once, been spent on earth.

And so it came to pass. Exactly one year later the Baal Shem Tov's blessing was fulfilled, and Schneur Zalman was born.

During the early years of Schneur Zalman's life, whenever Rabbi Boruch would make his semi-annual visits to the Baal Shem Tov, the latter would inquire about the young boy in great detail, giving special instructions regarding the care of the child.

* * *

On his third birthday, Rivkah and her sister-in-law, Devorah Leah, brought the boy to the Baal Shem Tov for the traditional "haircutting" ceremony.[6] The Baal Shem Tov cut off a few locks of hair, leaving *peyot* (side locks) according to custom, and he blessed the boy with the three-fold Priestly Blessing (Numbers 6:24-26). He then sent the visitors home, with his blessings for a safe journey and for the new year.

All the way home, little Schneur Zalman kept on asking his mother who the old Jew was who had cut his hair. "That was *Zaida* ('grandfather')," was her reply. Little did he then know that some day he would come to regard the Baal Shem Tov as his "grandfather" in a very real sense; namely, as the master of his master, Rabbi DovBer, the famed "Maggid of Mezritch," to whom he owed his spiritual fulfillment.

* * *

From his fifth birthday, Schneur Zalman began to display a phenomenal mental grasp in his Torah studies. Together with his insatiable thirst for knowledge, he experienced a great love for people. He revered Torah scholars for their scholarship, and he respected and loved ordinary folk for their simple faith and piety.

At first, little Schneur Zalman was tutored by local *melamdim*

---

6. According to this custom a Jewish boy receives his first haircut on, or soon after, his third birthday, when sidelocks (*peyot*) are left.

(teachers). After several years, in order to further develop his son's scholarship, Rabbi Baruch took him to the renowned teacher Rabbi Yissachar Ber of Kobilnik,[7] who lived in Lubavitch. Under Rabbi Yissachar Ber's tutelage the young scholar traversed the vast "Sea of the Talmud," and also familiarized himself with Kabbalah, the mystical, esoteric side of traditional Torah wisdom. In his spare time, the eager boy further expanded his knowledge through the study of mathematics, geometry, astronomy and philosophy. At the age of eleven, when Schneur Zalman solved one of the complicated mathematical problems posed in the Talmud, Rabbi Yissachar Ber sent for Rabbi Baruch and told the overjoyed father of his disciple: "There is nothing more that I can teach your son. He has grown beyond me."

Rabbi Baruch now took Schneur Zalman to Vitebsk, a center of Jewish Talmudic scholarship. The twelve year old boy won immediate recognition and fame as an "*iluy*," a genius, and he was accepted as an equal by the great scholars of the city. Eventually his fame reached Yehuda Leib Segal, a man of considerable wealth and scholarship, who wished to have him as his son-in-law. He approached Schneur Zalman's father and the match was duly arranged.

MARRIAGE AND THE EARLY YEARS

Rabbi Schneur Zalman was fifteen years old when he married Sterna. She was a worthy mate who stood by him throughout a lifetime of many tribulations.

The marriage was solemnized on Friday, the eve of *Shabbat Nachamu*, 5520 (1760). Rabbi Schneur Zalman had made it a condition of his consent to the marriage that the amount of 5,000 gold coins, which the father of the bride had promised by way of dowry, should be placed entirely at his, Rabbi Schneur Zalman's, disposal, to do with as he saw fit.

Within the first year of their marriage, Rabbi Schneur Zalman and his wife placed the entire amount in a fund to help Jewish fam-

---

7. Also known as Rabbi Yissachar Ber Kobilniker. He held the position of "Maggid" in Lubavitch. Subsequently he participated in Rabbi Schneur Zalman's communal activities. The latter loved and honored him as "the treasure of my heart and soul; a friend and brother he is to me."

ilies settle on land and engage in agricultural pursuits. They were aided in the acquisition of farmland and farming implements, in flour milling, spinning and weaving wool and linen, and in similar pursuits of livelihood. Thanks to this help many Jewish settlements sprang up in the vicinity of Vitebsk, along the banks of the Dvina River. Rabbi Schneur Zalman continued to preach publicly from time to time, encouraging Jews to give up peddling and take up instead some agricultural pursuit. He also visited the Jewish settlements and urged the Jewish farmers to arrange periodic study groups for the adults for the study of *Chumash, Midrash* and *Aggadah* on their own level.

* * *

Rabbi Schneur Zalman's prominent father-in-law, who had dealings with members of the local nobility, introduced his brilliant son-in-law to members of the nobility and high officialdom. Several episodes are related of Rabbi Schneur Zalman at that time, which greatly enhanced his reputation as a scientist among the local nobility. His acquaintance with the local nobility stood him in good stead in his work in behalf of his brethren, and in the crucial periods of his career.

* * *

By the time Rabbi Schneur Zalman was eighteen years old, thanks to his extraordinary assiduity and brilliance of mind, he had become "proficient in the entire Talmudic literature, with all its commentaries and early and late codifiers."[8] At the same time he studied the classics of Jewish philosophy and Kabbalah literature, especially the *Zohar* and the *Shenei Luchot Habrit (Shaloh)* of Rabbi Yeshaya Hurwitz.

Rabbi Schneur Zalman gathered around him a group of young men of excellent scholarship, and led them in the study of the Talmud as well as in the discipline of the Kabbalah. They organized a *minyan* (small congregation) and worshipped in the manner of the saintly *Shaloh*. For three years he led this group, and Rabbi Schneur

---

8. Preface to his *Shulchan Aruch*. On the testimony of his sons, who heard it from their father, Rabbi Schneur Zalman went through the entire Talmud with all early and late codifiers sixteen times by the time he was thirty years old, "studying on his feet, night and day."

Zalman's reputation as a brilliant scholar and teacher was further enhanced.

Rabbi Schneur Zalman had already conceived a new system of Divine service, based on the central principle that love of G-d and fear of G-d must derive from an intellectual approach, with a profound comprehension of the greatness of G-d. He also formulated the methods of attaining this end by the application of the principle "from my flesh I see G-d" (Job 19:26)—an inductive method leading from the microcosm (man) to the macrocosm (G-d)—and from the analogy of the soul powers in man to the Divine categories of the *Ein Sof,* using the attributes of the human soul as counterparts of the Divine categories. This system was eventually perfected in his *Likkutei Amarim Tanya.*

JOURNEY TO MEZRITCH

At the age of twenty, the brilliant young student left his home and family to search for satisfaction of an unfulfilled yearning in his soul. He felt that despite all of his knowledge, he was still missing an element of religious Jewish life—one that could not be captured in the solitude of the four walls of his own study. Two centers of Jewish learning and leadership then beckoned for his attention: Vilna, the main seat of Talmudic scholarship and fortress of the opposition to the young, yet rapidly growing Chasidic movement; and Mezritch, the seat of Rabbi DovBer, the Maggid of Mezritch, heir to the Baal Shem Tov's ideology and leadership of the Chasidic movement.

Right from the outset Rabbi Schneur Zalman realized that the sober, rationalistic atmosphere of Vilna and its scholars, headed by the Gaon Rabbi Eliyahu, could not offer him what he was searching for. Rabbi Schneur Zalman therefore chose to try Mezritch, where a new world beckoned; a place, it was said, that taught people how to pray.

Rabbi Schneur Zalman's decision to go to Mezritch aroused his father-in-law's vehement opposition, to the extent of depriving his daughter and son-in-law of any further financial support. But Rabbi Schneur Zalman's wife stood by him and agreed to his going there, provided that if he decided to stay, he would not extend his stay beyond eighteen months. She raised a little sum of money with which to buy a horse and cart for her husband's journey.

Soon after Pesach 5525 (1765), Rabbi Schneur Zalman left for Mezritch, accompanied by his brother Rabbi Yehuda Leib. Having made their way to Orsha, a distance of some fifty miles, the horse collapsed. On learning from his brother that the latter had left home without his wife's consent, Rabbi Schneur Zalman urged him to return, while he himself continued his journey to Mezritch on foot.

ENCOUNTER WITH THE MAGGID

Rabbi Schneur Zalman's first impression of the inner circle of disciples gathered about Rabbi DovBer of Mezritch was not very encouraging. He had expected a large academy brimming with sparkling personalities, scholars and wise men. Instead he found a group of unobtrusive people who, upon first sight, seemed to possess little that made seeking worthwhile. Nor was he particularly inspired by the pious admonitions which the Maggid of Mezritch addressed to the crowd that gathered in his synagogue. He was about to leave, when his eyes were opened to the true nature of the master and his inner circle.

Rabbi Schneur Zalman had decided to pay respects to the Maggid before returning to Liozna. He entered the master's house and stood among the crowd, when the eyes of Rabbi DovBer singled him out. They burrowed themselves deeply into the very abyss of Schneur Zalman's soul, exploring and evaluating its every quality. After a few minutes of pregnant silence the master not only told him what had been on his mind, but, without having been asked, gave Schneur Zalman an astoundingly simple yet convincing answer to two of three test questions which the young scholar had prepared in order to assure himself of a worthy master. Deeply impressed, Rabbi Schneur Zalman begged to be admitted into the inner circle of Rabbi DovBer's disciples.

A new world now unfolded itself before the eager eyes of the young scholar from Liozna, as he absorbed the Maggid's daily lectures on the teachings of the saintly Baal Shem Tov. In the company of such great men as Rabbi Nachum of Chernobyl, Rabbi Levi Yitzchak of Berditchev, Rabbi Elimelech of Lizensk, Rabbi Zusha of Anipoli, Rabbi Shmelke of Nikolsburg, his brother Rabbi Pinchas, and Rabbi Menachem Mendel of Vitebsk, he delved into the realm of holy teachings that unite G-d, Israel, the Torah and the world into one insoluble system of universal scope. The young son of Rabbi DovBer, Rabbi Avraham, who by his saintly conduct earned the title of *Malach* ("Angel"), was his guide to this higher sphere of wisdom and knowledge. In return, Rabbi Schneur Zalman instructed him in the realm of *halachah* (Jewish Law).

Thus the young *Rav* absorbed the fundamentals of Chasidism and found the satisfaction for the yearning in his soul that had driven him from his home and family.

THE RAV'S SHULCHAN ARUCH

Rabbi Schneur Zalman initially enjoyed little prestige among the established members of the Maggid's disciples. It would not be long, however, until Rabbi DovBer opened their eyes to his extraordinary qualities and revealed him to be a beacon of light for all of Israel.

In 5530 (1770), when Rabbi Schneur Zalman was barely twenty-five years old, Rabbi DovBer assigned him the task of re-editing the Code of Jewish Law, the *Shulchan Aruch*. It had been almost exactly two hundred years since Rabbi Yosef Caro had written his famous masterpiece. During this time much *halachic* material had been added in rabbinic literature, often giving rise to divergent opinions as to the practical application of the Jewish Law in given circumstances. It was Rabbi Schneur Zalman's task to examine and sift all of the new material, make decisions where necessary in the light of the earlier codifiers and Talmudic literature, and finally, embody the results into his new edition of the *Shulchan Aruch*, thus bringing it up-to-date. Needless to say, it was an enormous and responsible task, requiring extraordinary erudition and mastery of the entire Talmudic and *halachic* literature as well as a boldness to arbitrate and make decisions in disputed cases involving the opinions of the greatest masters of Jewish law up to his time. Rabbi Schneur Zalman superbly acquitted himself of this task, which at once immensely enhanced his reputation in the rabbinic world, and gave him an honored place among the great codifiers of Jewish law. The work became known as the "*Rav's Shulchan Aruch*," in distinction from its forerunner.[9]

---

9. Only *Hilchot Talmud Torah, Luach Birchat Hanehenin* and *Seder Birchat Hanehenin* were published in Rabbi Schneur Zalman's lifetime. The *Rav's Shulchan Aruch* in its entirety was first published posthumously, in 5576 (1816).

During this time Rabbi Schneur Zalman began to work on his system of Chabad philosophy, which was eventually embodied in his *Likkutei Amarim*, or *Tanya*. He worked on it intermittently for twenty years.

MAN OF MISSION

After the passing of the Maggid of Mezritch on the 19th day of *Kislev*, 5533 (1772), his disciples separated. Each one shouldered the task of propagating the movement of Chasidism in the country assigned to him by their late master. Rabbi Schneur Zalman inherited the most difficult of all missions. He was to capture the stronghold of opposition to the Chasidic movement, Lithuania, for the Chasidic ideology and way of life. This he was to accomplish in cooperation with Rabbi Menachem Mendel of Vitebsk, a senior disciple of the Maggid. No man of lesser stature as Talmudist could have undertaken such a job, for the opposition included some of the most illustrious scholars of the time.

Rabbi Schneur Zalman set out to acquaint himself more closely with the prevailing conditions in the very strongholds of the opposition. During the years 5532-35 (1772-75), he revisited such centers as Shklov, Minsk and Vilna, at times and in some places concealing his identity. Wherever possible he sowed the seeds of Chasidut, organized new Chasidic nuclei, and strengthened the movement in various communities.

Seeing that the opposition threatened to turn the conflict into an irreparable schism, Rabbi Schneur Zalman and his colleagues decided to do their best to avert it. In 5535 (1775), Rabbi Schneur Zalman accompanied his senior colleague, Rabbi Menachem Mendel, to Vilna in the hope of convincing Rabbi Eliyahu that his opposition to Chasidut was based on a misconception. Twice they unsuccessfully sought an audience with the Gaon, and when some influential community leaders persisted in their appeal to Rabbi Eliyahu to meet with the two leaders of the Chasidim, Rabbi Eliyahu left town and stayed away until the two emissaries had departed.

From Rabbi Schneur Zalman's own accounts of these efforts, it is clear that the weight of the opposition to the Chasidic movement, insofar as the Gaon of Vilna was concerned, rested on inaccurate, formal testimony presented to the Gaon by persons whom the Gaon had no reason to suspect of deliberate distortion. There were also certain deep-rooted philosophical and doctrinal differences which separated the Gaon of Vilna from the teachings of the Baal Shem Tov, particularly those expounded in the *Likkutei Amarim Tanya*.[10] These differences could have been resolved through a direct confrontation between the Gaon of Vilna and Rabbi Schneur Zalman, but this would never come to pass.

* * *

Throughout this period of time, Rabbi Schneur Zalman was actively engaged in preaching and disseminating the Chasidic doctrines according to his own interpretation. During his extensive travels many followers were attracted to him, not only from the masses but from the ranks of scholars as well. He established a school of selected disciples in his own town. The students were divided into three groups (*chadarim*) and many of them became distinguished scholars and Rabbis. The *chadarim*, established in Liozna during the years 5533-5538 (1773-1778), admitted only selected students of high scholastic ability for intensive studies of both Talmud and Chasidut. The faculty included, in addition to Rabbi Schneur Zalman himself, his three learned brothers, Rabbi Yehuda Leib, Rabbi Mordechai, and Rabbi Moshe. This academy of higher learning existed for twenty years, and produced Chasidic rabbis of outstanding caliber, who widely disseminated the Chabad doctrine.

PERSONAL CRISIS

In 5537 (1777), Rabbi Menachem Mendel of Vitebsk, with two of his colleagues, Rabbi Avraham of Kalisk and Rabbi Yisrael of Polotzk, together with a group of their followers, were due to leave for the Holy Land. Rabbi Schneur Zalman felt a great urge to join them and likewise emigrate to the Holy Land. By nature a peace-loving man, Rabbi Schneur Zalman did not cherish the battle which awaited him, and which he would have to wage single-handedly after his colleagues were gone. Moreover, he was imbued with a profound

---

10. Rabbi Eliyahu particularly objected to Rabbi Schneur Zalman's interpretation of the doctrine of *tzimtzum* (divine "contraction") and his concept of divine immanence. Apparently, the Gaon did not accept the Lurianic Kabbalah *in toto*, and interpreted some of its doctrines differently.

love for his fellow-Jews in general, and with deep respect and affection for Torah scholars in particular. The strife between the Mitnagdim and Chasidim was very painful to him, and seeing no prospects of immediate reconciliation and peace, he was sorely tempted to escape from it all.

He wrestled with the decision for three months. Finally, on *Chol Hamoed* Pesach, he announced that he would be joining his colleagues and leaving for the Holy Land immediately after Pesach.

In the beginning of the month of *Iyar*, Rabbi Schneur Zalman, with his family and his brothers, Rabbis Yehuda Leib, Mordechai and Moshe, and their families, as well as some of the disciples of the upper two *chadarim*, left Liozna, despite the pleadings of his followers. They made their way to Mohilev, on the Dniester River.

Rabbi Menachem Mendel of Vitebsk and Rabbi Avraham of Kalisk did not disguise their displeasure at their colleague's intention of abandoning his post. They urged him to reconsider his decision, asserting that he had no right to leave the land and thus deprive the Chasidim of his leadership at such a critical time. They also reminded him of the destiny which the Maggid of Mezritch had foreseen for him, with the assurance of the eventual success of his life's mission.

Rabbi Schneur Zalman spent three weeks in Mohilev in the company of his senior colleagues. During the last week of their sojourn together, Rabbi Schneur Zalman spent long hours each day in private discussions with Rabbi Menachem Mendel. They finally left without him, and he remained in Mohilev for two more weeks which he spent in seclusion. Then he let it be known that he would return to Lithuania.

In *Shevat* 5538 (1778), Rabbi Schneur Zalman finally returned to Liozna, amidst festive celebration.

By this time, the turbulence of anti-Chasidic agitation had abated considerably. The lull lasted for about three years. During this time Rabbi Schneur Zalman was able to concentrate his attention on his seminaries and on the dissemination of the teachings of Chasidut.

DEBATE IN MINSK

In the year 5543 (1783), an important disputation took place in Minsk between leading Mitnagdic *gaonim* from Vilna, Shklov, Brisk,

Minsk and Slutzk on one side, and Rabbi Schneur Zalman on the other. The debate, held in the public square, centered around Rabbi Schneur Zalman's philosophy, which was based on the teachings of the Baal Shem Tov—teachings that the Mitnagdim vehemently opposed.

Responding to the questions posed to him, Rabbi Schneur Zalman passionately and systematically outlined the basic doctrines of the Baal Shem Tov, demonstrating their veracity from genuine Torah sources and their place in mainstream Judaism.

According to eyewitness accounts, Rabbi Schneur Zalman's remarks, spoken with profound feeling and inspiration, left a tremendous impression on all present. Many who had come to witness the disputation in order to scoff at the head of the *kat* (sect), had been so inspired by his brilliant defense of the Baal Shem Tov's teachings that they were at once "converted."

It was said that four hundred followers, all of them distinguished Talmudic scholars, both young adults and elderly men, joined the Chasidic community, as a direct result of that disputation. Scores of young scholars followed Rabbi Schneur Zalman to Liozna.

COMMUNAL LEADER

Rabbi Schneur Zalman was a true leader, fully alive to the material needs of his brethren no less than to those of their spirit. Immediately after his wedding, as mentioned earlier, he began a campaign to induce more Jews to settle on the land and engage in agricultural pursuits. Rabbi Schneur Zalman devoted to this cause not only a great deal of effort, but also all of his financial resources.

From about the year 5532 (1772), Rabbi Schneur Zalman was engaged in an extensive plan to encourage large numbers of Jews living on the Russo-Polish border to move eastward, into the interior of Russia, where the economic opportunities were more promising.

Another one of Rabbi Schneur Zalman's devoted tasks was the raising of funds for the support of the newly established Chasidic settlements in the Holy Land. Incidentally, this campaign served as one of the bases for the calumny against him by his opponents, who denounced him as a traitor to the Russian government by accusing him of sending funds to the Turkish government. (The two countries were not on friendly terms at the time.)

When a decree was issued in 5568 (1808) for the expulsion of Jews living in rural areas and farms, depriving thousands of Jewish families of their means of livelihood, Rabbi Schneur Zalman embarked on an extensive fund-raising journey throughout Russia, aiming to meet the emergency and create the means for the financial rehabilitation of these unfortunate souls.

Rabbi Schneur Zalman carried on this communal work in addition to his daily tasks of advising and guiding his many followers who turned to him individually for all of their complicated problems. This was no small task, as he was credited with a personal following of some 100,000 Chasidim!

PHILOSOPHY AND PUBLICATION OF TANYA

During the years of struggle for the betterment of the spiritual life and economic conditions of his co-religionists, the *Rav* developed his magnificent philosophy of Chabad-Chasidism. Of the people who flocked about him after his return to Liozna, he demanded much more than the blind adherence required by the other schools of Chasidic thought. Whereas their ideology centered about the *Tzadik* as a person of supernatural powers, he posed the idea of the *Tzadik* mainly as a spiritual guide; a teacher rather than a miracle worker. The Chasid was to train himself for a life-task of faith and *avodah* —spiritual and moral "work"—which would carry him to the highest level of Chabad: "*chochmah*"—wisdom, "*binah*"—understanding, and "*daat*"—knowledge of the holiness of G-d, Israel and the Torah, forming a bond between heaven and earth.

Upon this basic thought Rabbi Schneur Zalman erected the mighty structure of Chabad ideology which aims for inner discipline and moral and intellectual progress towards the highest possible form of human existence and human achievement. This ideology was finally perfected and methodically formulated in Rabbi Schneur Zalman's *magnum opus*, the *Tanya*.

The first handwritten copies of essays and discourses that eventually became *Likkutei Amarim Tanya* began circulating among the Chasidim as early as 5552 (1792). Word spread quickly among the Chasidim that their Rebbe had written a work on practical, religious ethics, as a "guide" for the seekers of religious devotion. There was great demand for copies of this work.

Over the next few years, as circulation spread, copyists' errors began appearing in the text, and deliberate forgeries were made to cast Rabbi Shneur Zalman's philosophy in a negative light. In order to forestall any further tampering with the text by unscrupulous opponents, Rabbi Shneur Zalman finally consented to have the *Tanya* printed. The first edition was completed on the 20th of *Kislev*, 5557 (1796). It numbered 15,000 copies.

IMPRISONMENT AND VINDICATION

It was unavoidable that the man who went out to conquer Lithuania, the center of the opposition to the Chasidic movement, should meet with bitter hostility. His opponents resorted to the most extreme measures to undermine his work. Yet despite the violence and recklessness of the struggle, Rabbi Schneur Zalman never went beyond the limits of fairness and propriety. Like his revered master, the Maggid of Mezritch, he believed firmly in the inevitable victory of his cause, the propagation of Chasidism, without recourse to such disastrous steps as the reversing of a "*cherem*" (excommunication)[11] against the leaders of the opponents to Chasidism. When the men of Vilna used the "*cherem*" against the Chasidim, he still maintained his noble attitude and refused to respond in kind. He remained unmoved by the derision and even the open hostility of some of the other Chasidic leaders who urged him to answer the challenge with equal ferocity and ruthlessness.

His fairness, however, did not prevent his being denounced to the Russian government as a traitor and heretic. In 5559 (1798), a formal denunciation was submitted before the authorities in Petersburg, accusing Rabbi Schneur Zalman and other leading Chasidim of activities inimical to the Czar and the country. Czar Paul lost no time in ordering the governor of the White Russian province to arrest Rabbi Schneur Zalman and send him under heavy guard to Petersburg. An order was also sent to the governor of Lithuania to investigate the charges, which had originated in Vilna, and to have the leaders of the conspirators brought to the capital under the most stringent precautionary measures.

---

11. According to Jewish law, an unjustly pronounced "*cherem*" may be turned back upon the pronouncers of the ban.

In the autumn of 5559 (1798), on the day after the Festival of Simchat Torah (the 24th day of *Tishrei*), Rabbi Schneur Zalman was arrested and taken under heavy armed guard from Liozna to Petersburg. He was placed in the Peter-Paul fortress, pending an investigation by the Secret Imperial Council, which was to present its report to the Senate for judgment. At the same time twenty-two of Rabbi Schneur Zalman's followers in Vilna were also arrested, of whom seven were brought to Petersburg, to await trial on charges of conspiracy and high treason.

The arrest of their leader threw panic into the hearts of the Chasidim.

Rabbi Schneur Zalman's calm composure was extraordinary. It was not a passive resignation to overpowering forces that was reflected in his demeanor, but rather a firm determination to meet a challenge which would put his leadership and all that he stood for to the supreme test. He was determined to pave the road of self-sacrifice for the Chasidic ideals and way of life, a road which he knew his successors and followers would have to tread time and again.

On the following day, it being a Friday, when six hours were left to the time of lighting the Shabbat candles, the prisoner requested the officer in charge to halt the journey until after the termination of the Shabbat. The officer refused to accede to the request. The next moment an axle of the carriage broke. Undismayed, the officer sent for repairmen who were brought from the nearest village. The axle was repaired, but when they were ready to proceed, one of the horses collapsed and died. The dead horse was replaced by a fresh horse from the village. However, strangely enough, the horses could not budge the carriage. The officer was now convinced that this was no ordinary situation. In a more conciliatory mood, the officer suggested to his prisoner that they proceed only as far as the nearby village and rest there. The Rebbe refused to proceed any further. However, he permitted the carriage to be turned off the highway into the adjacent field. There he spent the Shabbat.

* * *

Many interesting episodes are told about Rabbi Schneur Zalman's imprisonment in the Peter-Paul fortress. One such episode:

The chief investigator who visited Rabbi Schneur Zalman in his cell to interrogate him, was greatly impressed with the prisoner, who, obviously, was no ordinary rebel. This high official was a man of higher education, and was also well versed in the Bible. On one occasion the interrogator asked the prisoner the meaning of the biblical verse, "And G-d called unto Adam, and said to him, 'Where are you?'" (Genesis 3:9). Did not G-d know where Adam was?

Rabbi Schneur Zalman explained the text in the light of the biblical commentaries, particularly that of Rashi, that it was in a manner of opening the conversation, so as not to overwhelm the man who was cowering in fear of punishment.

The interrogator replied that he was aware of this explanation, but wondered if the prisoner had something more profound to say on this question.

Thereupon, Rabbi Schneur Zalman asked the official if he believed in the eternal truth of the Holy Scriptures, and that the contents of the Holy Book had validity for all times and all individuals.

The official replied that he did so believe.

It was immensely gratifying to the prisoner to know that his investigator was a G-d-fearing man, and he proceeded to explain the text to him in the following terms:

The question which G-d asked the first man, "Where are you?", is an eternal divine call to each and every man, demanding constantly, "Where do you stand?" Every man is allotted a certain number of years and days to live on this earth, so that he may fulfill his duty to G-d and to his fellow man every day, and every year. And so the divine call goes out every day to each and every individual, demanding introspection and self-examination as to his standing and station in life. For example, you are so many years old (he mentioned the exact age of the official). Ask yourself: What have you accomplished in all these years? How much good have you done?…

The official was amazed that the sage should have divined his exact age. He was also deeply impressed by the meaningful explanation. He questioned the sage further on various matters pertaining to the Jewish faith, to which Rabbi Schneur Zalman replied point by point with extraordinary wisdom and erudition. The stunned official exclaimed, "This is truly divine!"

Another interesting episode is related as follows:

Czar Paul, sensitive to anything that smacked of rebellion, was personally intrigued by the Jewish rebel accused of high treason. He was even more intrigued by the account of the chief investigator, who reported to him on the progress of the investigation. According to this account, the prisoner was a man of exceptional wisdom and saintliness, a man of the spirit, who was not likely to be involved in a conspiracy against the Emperor. The Czar was very curious to meet this extraordinary person. He decided to visit him incognito in his cell.

Disguised as one of the investigators, the Czar entered the prisoner's cell, whereupon the prisoner rose to his feet and, with the respect accorded to royalty, greeted the visitor with a benediction.

Asked to explain his conduct, the Rebbe declared, "Our Sages state that kingship on earth is a replica of the Kingship in Heaven. When Your Imperial Majesty entered, I felt a sense of awe and trembling such as I have not experienced with any of the officials that have visited here. I knew you were the Czar in person."

* * *

On Tuesday, the 19th of *Kislev*,[12] 5559 (1798), fifty-three days[13] after his arrest, and following an intense investigation of the charges which included intense interrogation, Rabbi Schneur Zalman was informed that he had been found innocent of the charges, and was released. Moreover, the Chasidic movement was officially sanctioned by the authorities and permitted to carry on its practices as before. Simultaneously an order was sent to Governor Bulgakov of Lithuania to release all twenty-two Jews imprisoned in Vilna, who had been held there pending the outcome of the investigation of their leader. By order of Czar Paul they were to be released at once, "since nothing was found in the conduct of the Jews belonging to the

---

12. Rabbi Schneur Zalman considered the day auspicious, since it is the anniversary of the demise of his master Rabbi DovBer, the Maggid of Mezritch, twenty-six years previously. (A *Yahrzeit* is considered auspicious by Chasidim because it is believed that on that day the soul of the departed ascends to a higher level in the heavenly spheres.)

13. Chabad Chasidim consider this number significant, as it corresponds to the number of chapters in the *Tanya*.

Chasidic movement that was inimical to the State, nor anything that might be considered as depravity, or disturbance to the general peace."

The news of the Rebbe's release electrified the Chasidim, whose joy was indescribable.

Thus came into being the historic festival of *Yud-Tet* (19th) *Kislev*, the anniversary of the liberation of the founder of Chabad, and the day immortalized as the *Rosh Hashanah* of Chasidut.

SECOND ARREST

Hardly two years later, in the spring of 5560 (1800), the extreme opposition led by the spiteful Avigdor Chaimovitch of Pinsk once again denounced Rabbi Schneur Zalman as a traiter and heritic before the government in Petersburg, lodging a complaint to the Czar. In the autumn of that year, after several months of investigations carried out by various jurisdictions, the Attorney General finally issued the order to again apprehend Rabbi Schneur Zalman. Once again he was brought to the Russian capital and imprisoned, this time facing nineteen charges fabricated by Chaimovitch. But, as before, he was able to convincingly answer all of the questions directed toward him, and was cleared of all guilt. After being under arrest for less than three weeks, he was released on Chanukah, 5561 (1800), with the approval of Czar Alexander I, who shared the admiration of his predecessor for the venerable leader of the Lithuanian Chasidic movement.[14] He was, however, ordered to remain in the capital.

Rabbi Schneur Zalman spent another seven months in Petersburg, answering Chaimovitch's repeated appeals and subsequently submitting his own petition to the Czar for a restraining order protecting him and the Chasidim from future slander by Chaimovitch. After lodging two such petitions, Rabbi Schneur Zalman finally left the capital on the 11th of *Menachem Av*.

He did not, however, return to Liozna. At the invitation of Prince Lubomirsky, a prominent nobleman and estate owner of White Russia who had been greatly impressed with the venerable

---

14. In 1991, the Russian government released all of the files pertaining to Rabbi Schneur Zalman's indictment and interrogation. They were subsequently published in *Kerem Chabad*, vol. 4.

Jewish leader, and who perhaps was not unmindful of the benefits the latter might bring to his estates, Rabbi Schneur Zalman agreed to take up residence in the town of Liadi, one of Lubomirsky's possessions. The prince provided a fine carriage for the Rebbe with two mounted guards. Accompanied by an entourage of close Chasidim, in four additional carriages, augmented on the way by thousands of followers (according to one report the number was about 5,000), Rabbi Schneur Zalman arrived in Liadi on the eve of *Shabbat Nachamu*, the 14th of *Menachem Av*, 5561 (1801). Here Rabbi Schneur Zalman spent the remainder of his life—more than a decade—and became known as the "*Rav* of Liadi."

FINAL JOURNEY

Rabbi Schneur Zalman was not destined to end his life in peace. In 1812, Napoleon invaded Russia, and the route of the invasion led through White Russia. The Jewish leader, who had twice been accused of high treason, turned out to be a most loyal patriot. Although the French conqueror was hailed in some religious Jewish quarters as the harbinger of a new era of political and economic freedom, Rabbi Schneur Zalman, to whom the ultimate criteria were spiritual rather than economic or political, saw in Napoleon a threat to basic religious principles and spiritual values. He urged his numerous followers to help the Russian war effort against the invaders in every possible way. With the aid of his followers behind the enemy lines, some of whom were employed by the French Military Command, Rabbi Schneur Zalman was also able to render valuable intelligence to the Russian generals at the front.

When the French armies approached Liadi, the Russian generals advised Rabbi Schneur Zalman to flee. On the 29th of *Menachem Av*, 5572 (1812), Rabbi Schneur Zalman hastily left Liadi, leaving everything behind, and fled with his family towards Smolensk. No sooner did the refugees reach Smolensk than they had to continue their flight in the face of the advancing invader. For some five months Rabbi Schneur Zalman and his family suffered the hardships and perils of the road and of an unusually inclement winter, until they reached Piena, a small village in the district of Kursk. Here the aged Rabbi succumbed to a severe illness which he contracted in the final stages of the harrowing journey. After the close of Shabbat, the eve of the 24th of *Tevet,* 5573 (1812), Rabbi Schneur Zalman passed away at the age of sixty-eight. He was laid to rest in the Jewish cemetery of Haditch, near the city of Poltava. Chasidic tradition has taken note of Rabbi Schneur Zalman's life-span, pointing out that sixty-eight is the numerical equivalent of the Hebrew word *chayim* ("life").

EPILOGUE

Thus came to an end the eventful and productive life of Rabbi Schneur Zalman. It was a life sadly harassed to the end by events and circumstances beyond his control, but never lacking in inner peace and harmony.

Rabbi Schneur Zalman was a man of many colorful facets, all harmoniously complementing each other. The rationalist and mystic, the Kabbalist and Talmudist, the saint and the man of the world, the humble worshipper and the sagacious leader—all were harmoniously blended together into the unique personality of Rabbi Schneur Zalman, and each coming forcefully to the fore as the occasion demanded. He was known to attain the loftiest heights of mystical communion, so that in moments of ecstasy during prayer he could batter his knuckles against the wall to the point of bleeding (his disciples eventually affixed a soft pad on the wall), yet he would hear the cry of a child next door and interrupt his meditation or study to comfort it. Knowing as he did the consuming bliss of soulful devotion, he was heard to exclaim, "I do not want Your Paradise, I do not want Your World-to-Come; I want only You, You alone!" Yet he could tear himself away from his supernal state in order to find time to receive and console a stricken widow, or help a poor innkeeper thrown out into the road for lack of rent. He was a humble and peace-loving man, humble enough to disclaim any originality for his philosophic system, and conciliatory towards his adversaries. Yet he was indomitable and ready to suffer martyrdom for his ideals and convictions.

These characteristics were in Rabbi Schneur Zalman more than natural traits of a noble character. They were the embodiment of his philosophic system, of which the "supremacy of spirit over matter" was a basic principle. He was not an abstract philosopher or moralist whose mind floated in a world of pure speculation; he truly practiced what he preached. He lived with his people and for his people, and this, perhaps more than anything else, accounts for the tremendous following which he had acquired in his lifetime.

The Chabad ideology and way of life which Rabbi Schneur Zalman introduced more than two centuries ago has well withstood the test of time. The Chabad system has not been shaken by all the transilience which characterizes the last two centuries of the history of mankind at large, and of the Jewish people in particular. Chabad today is as vigorous and dynamic a force in Jewish life as it ever was.

IMPORTANT DATES

IMPORTANT DATES IN THE LIFE OF
RABBI SCHNEUR ZALMAN OF LIADI
THE ALTER REBBE

5505 (1745): Birth of the Alter Rebbe, Rabbi Schneur Zalman, to Rabbi Baruch and his wife Rivkah, daughter of Rabbi Avraham, on 18 *Elul.* At his Bar Mitzvah celebration, the greatest scholars of the generation entitled him *Rav tanna upalig* ("He is equal in stature to the scholars of previous generations, and is entitled to disagree with them").

5520 (1760): Marries Rebbetzin Sterna. Launches a vigorous campaign—with personal effort and with his own funds—to encourage Jews to take up farming.

5524 (1764): His first visit to Mezritch.

5527 (1767): Accepts post of *Maggid* ("Preacher") of Liozna.

5530 (1770): Begins compiling the *Shulchan Aruch [HaRav].*

5532 (1772): Defines the doctrine of Chabad-Chasidut; begins campaign for Jews living in the Vitebsk area to move across the frontier into Russia.

5533-5538 (1773-1778): Establishes *Yeshivah* in Liozna, known as *Cheder* I, II and III.

5534 (1774): Travels to Vilna with Rabbi Menachem Mendel of Vitebsk to meet the Gaon of Vilna. The Gaon refuses to meet with them.

5537 (1777): Accompanies Rabbi Menachem Mendel on the first stage of his journey to the Holy Land, as far as the city of Mogilev, on the Dniester River.

5543 (1783): Engages in the great disputation in Minsk and emerges victorious.

5551 (1791): His writings on Talmud, *Halachah* and Chasidut are widely disseminated.

5554 (1794): Publishes *Hilchot Talmud Torah* ("Laws of Torah Study").

5557 (1796): Publishes *Tanya*.

5559 (1798): Arrested on the day after Sukkot; released on 19 *Kislev*.

5561 (1800): Summoned to Petersburg on the day after Sukkot; on the following 11 *Menachem Av* (1801) he leaves Petersburg directly for Liadi, Mogilev Province.

5572 (1812): Leaves Liadi on the eve of *Shabbat Mevarchim Elul.* After wandering with his family and many Chasidim, he arrives in the village of Piena, Kursk Province, on 12 *Tevet* 5573 (1812). There, after Shabbat ends, on the eve of Sunday, 24 *Tevet*, he passes away. He is interred in Haditch, Poltava Province.

His wife: Rebbetzin Sterna, daughter of the magnate Rabbi Yehuda Leib Segal and his wife Baila.

His daughters: Rebbetzin Freida; married Rabbi Eliyahu, son of Rabbi Mordechai.
Rebbetzin Devorah Leah; married Rabbi Shalom Shachna, son of Rabbi Noach.
Rebbetzin Rachel; married Rabbi Avraham son of Rabbi Tzvi Sheines.

His sons: The Rebbe, Rabbi DovBer.
Rabbi Chaim Avraham.
Rabbi Moshe.

His sister: Rebbetzin Sara.

His brothers-in-law:
Rabbi Yisrael, known as Reb Yisrael Kazak, married to Rebbetzin Sara.
Rabbi Akiva Fradkin of Shklov, married to Rebbetzin Sterna's sister.

PUBLISHED WORKS

PUBLISHED WORKS OF RABBI SCHNEUR ZALMAN

1. *Hilchot Talmud Torah*
2. *Birchot Hanehenin*
3. *Tanya and Mehadura Kama of Tanya*
4. *Siddur*
5. *Shulchan Aruch*
6. *Sefer Shaalot U'Teshuvot*
7. *Biurei Hazohar*
8. *Torah Or*
9. *Likkutei Torah*
10. *Bonei Yerushalayim*
11. *Maamarei Admur Hazaken, 24 vol.*
12. *Igrot Kodesh, 2 vol.*

Translations:
The Tanya has been translated into the following languages: Yiddish, English, French, Italian, Spanish, Arabic, Russian, Portuguese and German. A Braille edition is also available.

OTHER TITLES IN
THE CHASIDIC HERITAGE SERIES

THE ETERNAL BOND *from Torah Or*

By Rabbi Schneur Zalman of Liadi
Translated by Rabbi Ari Sollish

This discourse explores the spiritual significance of *brit milah*, analyzing two dimensions in which our connection with G-d may be realized. For in truth, there are two forms of spiritual circumcision: Initially, man must "circumcise his heart," freeing himself to the best of his ability from his negative, physical drives; ultimately, though, it is G-d who truly liberates man from his material attachment.

≤ò ≤ò ≤ò

JOURNEY OF THE SOUL from *Torah Or*

By Rabbi Schneur Zalman of Liadi
Translated by Rabbi Ari Sollish

Drawing upon the parallel between Queen Esther's impassioned plea to King Ahasuerus for salvation and the soul's entreaty to G-d for help in its spiritual struggle, this discourse examines the root of the soul's exile, and the dynamics by which it lifts itself from the grip of materiality and ultimately finds a voice with which to express its G-dly yearnings. Includes a brief biography of the author.

· ≤ò ≤ò ≤ò

TRANSFORMING THE INNER SELF from *Likkutei Torah*

By Rabbi Schneur Zalman of Liadi
Translated by Rabbi Ari Sollish

This discourse presents a modern-day perspective on the Biblical command to offer animal sacrifices. Rabbi Schneur Zalman teaches that each of us possesses certain character traits that can be seen as "animalistic," or materialistic, in nature, which can lead a person toward a life of material indulgence. Our charge, then, is to "sacrifice" and transform the animal within, to refine our animal traits and utilize them in our pursuit of spiritual perfection.

≤ò ≤ò ≤ò

FLAMES from *Gates of Radiance*
By Rabbi DovBer of Lubavitch
Translated by Dr. Naftoli Loewenthal

This discourse focuses on the multiple images of the lamp, the oil, the wick and the different hues of the flame in order to express profound guidance in the divine service of every individual. Although *Flames* is a Chanukah discourse, at the same time, it presents concepts that are of perennial significance. Includes the first English biography of the author ever published.

∽⊰∽⊰∽⊰

THE MITZVAH TO LOVE YOUR FELLOW AS YOURSELF from *Derech Mitzvotecha*
By Rabbi Menachem Mendel of Lubavitch, the Tzemach Tzedek
Translated by Rabbis Nissan Mangel and Zalman Posner

The discourse discusses the Kabbalistic principle of the "collective soul of the world of *Tikkun*" and explores the essential unity of all souls. The discourse develops the idea that when we connect on a soul level, we can love our fellow as we love ourselves; for in truth, we are all one soul. Includes a brief biography of the author.

∽⊰∽⊰∽⊰

TRUE EXISTENCE *Mi Chamocha 5629*
By Rabbi Shmuel of Lubavitch
Translated by Rabbis Yosef Marcus and Avraham D. Vaisfiche

This discourse revolutionizes the age-old notion of Monotheism, i.e., that there is no other god besides Him. Culling from Talmudic and Midrashic sources, the discourse makes the case that not only is there no other god besides Him, there is nothing besides Him—literally. The only thing that truly exists is G-d. Includes a brief biography of the author.

∽⊰∽⊰∽⊰

TRUE EXISTENCE *The Chasidic View of Reality*

A Video-CD with Rabbi Manis Friedman

Venture beyond science and Kabbalah and discover the world of Chasidism. This Video-CD takes the viewer step-by-step through the basic chasidic and kabbalistic view of creation and existence. In clear, lucid language, Rabbi Manis Friedman deciphers these esoteric concepts and demonstrates their modern-day applications.

‸‸‸

YOM TOV SHEL ROSH HASHANAH 5659
Discourse One

By Rabbi Shalom DovBer of Lubavitch
Translated by Rabbis Yosef Marcus and Moshe Miller

The discourse explores the attribute of *malchut* and the power of speech while introducing some of the basic concepts of Chasidism and Kabbalah in a relatively easy to follow format. Despite its title and date of inception, the discourse is germane throughout the year. Includes a brief biography of the author.

‸‸‸

FORCES IN CREATION
Yom Tov Shel Rosh Hashanah 5659 Discourse Two

By Rabbi Shalom DovBer of Lubavitch
Translated by Rabbis Moshe Miller and Shmuel Marcus

This is a fascinating journey beyond the terrestrial, into the myriad spiritual realms that shape our existence. In this discourse, Rabbi Shalom DovBer systematically traces the origins of earth, Torah and souls, drawing the reader higher and higher into the mystical, cosmic dimensions that lie beyond the here and now, and granting a deeper awareness of who we are at our core.

‸‸‸

THE PRINCIPLES OF
EDUCATION AND GUIDANCE
Klalei Hachinuch Vehahadrachah
By Rabbi Yosef Yitzchak of Lubavitch
Translated by Rabbi Y. Eliezer Danzinger

The Principles of Education and Guidance is a compelling treatise that examines the art of educating. In this thought provoking analysis, Rabbi Yosef Yitzchak teaches how to assess the potential of any pupil, how to objectively evaluate one's own strengths, and how to successfully use reward and punishment—methods that will help one become a more effective educator.

∾∾∾

THE FOUR WORLDS
By Rabbi Yosef Yitzchak of Lubavitch
Translated by Rabbis Yosef Marcus and Avraham D. Vaisfiche
Overview by Rabbi J. Immanuel Schochet

At the core of our identity is the desire to be one with our source, and to know the spiritual realities that give our physical life the transcendental importance of the Torah's imperatives. In this letter to a yearning Chasid, the Rebbe explains the mystical worlds of Atzilut, Beriah, Yetzira, and Asiya.

∾∾∾

ONENESS IN CREATION
By Rabbi Yosef Yitzchak of Lubavitch
Translated by Rabbi Y. Eliezer Danzinger

Said by Rabbi Yosef Yitzchak at the close of his 1930 visit to Chicago, this discourse explores the concept of Divine Unity as expressed in the first verse of the Shema. The discourse maintains that it is a G-dly force that perpetually sustains all of creation. As such, G-d is one with creation. And it is our study of Torah and performance of the mitzvot that reveals this essential oneness.

∾∾∾

GARMENTS OF THE SOUL
Vayishlach Yehoshua 5736

By Rabbi Menachem M. Schneerson, the Lubavitcher Rebbe
Translated by Rabbi Yosef Marcus

Often what is perceived in this world as secondary is in reality most sublime. What appears to be mundane and inconsequential is often most sacred and crucial. Thus at their source, the garments of the human, both physical and spiritual, transcend the individual.

⳯ ⳯ ⳯

THE UNBREAKABLE SOUL
Mayim Rabbim 5738

By Rabbi Menachem M. Schneerson, the Lubavitcher Rebbe
Translated by Rabbi Ari Sollish

The discourse begins with an unequivocal declaration: No matter how much one may be inundated with materialism, the flame of the soul burns forever. This discourse speaks to one who finds pleasure in the material world, yet struggles to find spirituality in his or her life.

⳯ ⳯ ⳯

ON THE ESSENCE OF CHASIDUS
Kunteres Inyana Shel Toras Hachasidus

By Rabbi Menachem M. Schneerson, the Lubavitcher Rebbe

In this landmark discourse, the Lubavitcher Rebbe, Rabbi Menachem M. Schneerson, explores the contribution of Chasidus to a far deeper and expanded understanding of Torah. The Rebbe analyzes the relationship Chasidus has with Kabbalah, the various dimensions of the soul, the concept of Moshiach and the Divine attributes—all in this slim volume.

⳯ ⳯ ⳯

THERE ARE MANY IMPORTANT MANUSCRIPTS THAT
ARE READY TO GO TO PRESS, BUT ARE
WAITING FOR A SPONSOR LIKE YOU.

PLEASE CONSIDER ONE OF THESE OPPORTUNITIES
AND MAKE AN EVERLASTING CONTRIBUTION TO
JEWISH SCHOLARSHIP AND CHASIDIC LIFE.

FOR MORE INFORMATION PLEASE CONTACT:

THE CHASIDIC HERITAGE SERIES
770 EASTERN PARKWAY
BROOKLYN, NEW YORK 11213
TEL: 718.774.4000
E-MAIL: INFO@KEHOTONLINE.COM

COMING SOON!

YOM TOV SHEL ROSH HASHANAH 5659
Discourse Three
By Rabbi Shalom DovBer of Lubavitch
Translated by Rabbi Y. Eliezer Danzinger

⊰⊰⊰

HACHODESH 5700
By Rabbi Yosef Yitzchak of Lubavitch
Translated by Rabbi Yosef Marcus

⊰⊰⊰

VE'ATAH TETZAVEH 5741
By Rabbi Menachem M. Schneerson, the Lubavitcher Rebbe
Translated by Rabbi Yosef Marcus

⊰⊰⊰